GRAND FINISHES FOR

Tile

Also by Matt Nikitas

Grand Finishes for Carpentry

Grand Finishes for Walls and Floors

GRAND FINISHES FOR

Tile

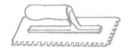

Home Installation Projects 101

Matt Nikitas

Illustrations by Amy Evans and Matt Nikitas

Inside Photographs by Ronald Monk

ST. MARTIN'S GRIFFIN ▓ NEW YORK

www.stmartins.com

Illustrations by Amy Evans and Matt Nikitas
Interior photos by Ron Monk
Used with permission

Book design by Jessica Shatan

ISBN 0-312-27700-8

First Edition: October 2001

10 9 8 7 6 5 4 3 2 1

This book is dedicated to
Hampton Coley.

CONTENTS

With Special Thanks to . . .

Cleo and W. Austin Barrett, Brian Leahy, Christus Nikitas, Jeannetta Coley, Dan Waters, Alison Lazarus; Devlin, Brian John, and Humphrey; Ronnie Monk, Ron Chisenhall, Amy Evans, Joe Cleemann, Mike Nikitas (*the talented and charismatic anchor of Boston's NECN*), Jon Blieberg, and especially Matthew Canton. I am also grateful for the overwhelming support I received from the publication of my two previous efforts at offering home improvement help, especially from the impartial and wonderfully astute readers Diamond and Angela Nikitas (*now, if I could just get over and repair their popcorn ceiling . . .*).

GRAND FINISHES FOR

Tile

History of Tiling

IN THE BILLIONS OF YEARS THAT THE EARTH HAS developed, no animal organism is older or has changed as little over the millennia than the insect. Many species began mixing paste and dirt to build their abodes. And within all the artifacts found regarding man, every indication leads us to think that since even before what records indicate, man has mixed sand and clay and other earth-bound ingredients to create a cement or mortar as a solid surface to protect himself from the elements. On the island now known as Crete, we have records from as early as 18th century B.C. of brickmakers having overlaid clay and mud, and mixed it into a mortar, to house themselves and others . . . not too long after they emerged from the cave.

Soon enough man found that placing this mixture out in the sun made the mixture much denser and it lasted much longer. The *firing* of bricks to make the mixed block hard and useful as a building product was perfected as early as 4000 B.C. Evidence of almost *universal* brick-making techniques has been found in African, Asian, and the Mediterranean countries. As Charlton Heston was forced to do in *The Ten Commandments,* straw and clay was first mixed with mud by hand and foot. It was then formed, crudely at first and then with more precision as the centuries passed, into various-sized bricks and blocks that were baked (*fired*) to increase the density and strength and make them suitable for building. In arid countries like Egypt the first firing technique involved placing the blocks and tiles in the sun, then by baking them in a fired kiln, an oven similar to the ones used for baking bread, but larger.

As I mentioned in my last book, *Grand Finishes for Carpentry,* wood moldings first originated in stone that was set and used for ornamental construction. But mixing and setting stone for housing and shelter started much further back. Several thousand years B.C. as humans became more civilized, they began to get creative with the fired building material, decorating it and making it more pleasing to the eye. First colored and glazed with copper, other colors and dyes were soon incorporated to make them more varied and decorative.

By 900 B.C. ceramic tile had been simultaneously developed in all areas of China, Persia (Iran), Spain, the Netherlands, and Turkey. Ceramics used for building materials as well as pottery were found in Mesopotamia (Iraq) as early as 4000 B.C. with white and blue strips. Chinese stoneware, decorated with white glazing, has been found from as early as 1500 B.C., during the Shang-Yin Dynasty.

Since tiles were being designed, modified, and

The Voice of Experience

At the turn of the *last* century (1900), Zanesville, Ohio, was producing more tile than any other place on earth. *(Besides that, the first "highway" was developed here.)* Geologically, it sits right smack in the middle of large clay deposits, and even though they don't put out nearly as much tile as they did a hundred years ago, residents still identify their town as something of a pottery capital, and hold annual festivals to display their wares.

used long before anyone recorded language with writing, it's difficult to say who or what people first uttered a word to mean *tile.* Yet the craft of using them for exterior and interior building materials seemed to grow simultaneously throughout the world. Today, though, we know the word we use is a prehistoric word borrowed from Latin *tegular,* meaning a flat or curved piece of clay, stone, concrete, or other material, especially used for roofs, floors, walls. According to *Webster's Dictionary* the word "ceramic" comes from the Greek *keramikos,* or "potter's clay," and is "the art of making useful or ornamental objects from clay by shaping them and firing them at high temperatures."

An enduring form of tilemaking, which was also applied to the manufacture of vases and other cooking and decorative stoneware, is *terra-cotta,* which is from the Italian meaning "baked earth." This method of hard-baked clay, either in its natural reddish-brown color or painted or glazed, was perfected and utilized through Persia, predynastic Egypt, China, and Assyria (Syria). Terracotta roof tiles are still very much in use in warm climates like Florida and the Southwestern areas of our country, as well as in the Mediterranean countries of Greece, Italy, and Turkey.

Reaching its height in the 6th century, was the art of Mosaics, in which stone, bits of glass, even semiprecious stone and small pieces of marble were incorporated into a larger slab of mortar or marble to create a design or picture. Set, displayed, and used as floors, walls, and ceilings, mosaics were commissioned in houses of worship in Turkey, Russia, and Greece.

Tile jobs are divided into two kinds of applications: a **wet installation** and a **non-wet** or **dry installation.** You can probably guess that a wet installation would be walls inside a bathtub or

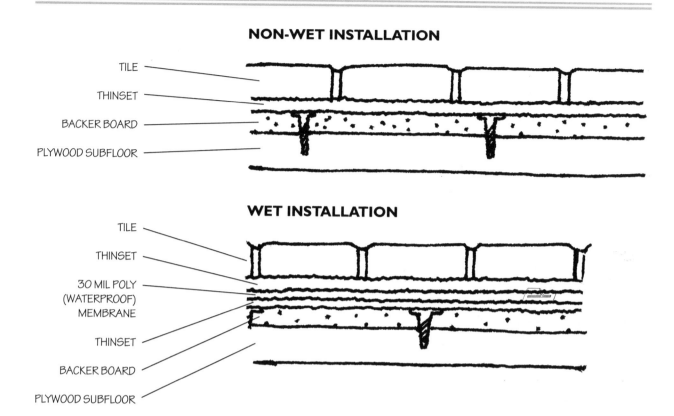

NON-WET INSTALLATION

TILE
THINSET
BACKER BOARD
PLYWOOD SUBFLOOR

WET INSTALLATION

TILE
THINSET
30 MIL POLY
(WATERPROOF)
MEMBRANE
THINSET
BACKER BOARD
PLYWOOD SUBFLOOR

shower, a floor in a bathroom and possibly in a kitchen, or, specifically, a kitchen counter. A non-wet area would be elsewhere in the house, like an entryway, hall, or even a water closet that is used primarily for guests: any surface that won't be exposed to continual water and moisture.

Though I don't plan to use these two words again in this book, vitreous and nonvitreous,

applies to the amount of water a tile absorbs. A vitreous tile absorbs from 0% to 3% water, semi-vitreous tile absorbs up to 7% water, and non-vitreous (*like patio tiles and other unglazed, low-fired tiles*) can absorb over 7%. It probably won't come up, but you never know: the seller might be impressed by your choice of words when you're shopping for new tile.

Some Vocabulary Words

THE UNDERLAYMENT REFERS TO THE SURFACE onto which you are putting the tiles directly. Also called the **substrate,** it can describe the complete cross-section of layers that were installed specifically for the tile application, or just the immediate surface on which the adhesive is put. Though mortar and thinset

could be considered the same product, **mortar** generally refers to the mud or bed laid as a substrate by many tradesmen, and I'll go into that more at the end of Chapter 1.

A **thick bed installation** refers to the traditional mortar bed over the plywood or concrete subfloor. What we'll focus on mainly in this book will be the **thin bed installation**, which will consist of only the **thinset** (*adhesive mortar*) being used to bed the tiles. I will also tell you about the **latex additive**, a milky liquid substance that is used for a variety of purposes. I'll go into detail later in this chapter for the uses of all these products.

Durability of a Tiled Surface

THEY OBVIOUSLY LAST: CHURCHES AND TEMples thousands of years old are testimony to that. (*Actually another Charlton Heston film comes to mind when illustrating the resilience of tile: In* Beneath the Planet of Apes—*the first movie had already established that the ape planet was Earth in the future—James Franciscus came across tiled areas of the New York City subway system. The mosaics spelling out "Times Square" and "Grand Central Station" were still visible after several thousand years and a nuclear holocaust. Though fiction, this scenario fairly represents how tenacious a tiled application can be. We have many examples throughout the world of stone, mortar, and tiled surfaces that have survived may millennia.*) Tiling floors and walls are still seen today as a long-lasting and wonderful way to finish a surface. Once grouted and sealed, you can splash water on them or wash them and they will hold up. I mean, you can't line the inside of your shower with oak planks, right? And a tiled surface *should* hold up.

If it is done right. One of my tile-installer heros, whose books and videos have been reference material for me and my crew over the years, once said that if a tile installation is going to last it will depend 100% on preparation. Though I tend to think the spread might be closer to 82% (*I give the 18% to the installation of the tile itself: how thickly or thinly the adhesive was spread, for instance*), his point is well taken. He was trying to say that it almost never happens that the tile itself is at fault. When a tile job fails (*the tile may crack or loosen, the grout starts to show hairline cracks, then water gets in and weakens the underlayment further . . .*) it is almost always the result of a poorly prepared and installed surface.

Available Styles and Sizes of Tiles: Natural Stone, Slate, Ceramic, Marble, Granite

THERE IS SO MUCH GREAT STUFF AVAILABLE today! The vast majority of tiles for floors and walls marketed are machine-processed (*all dependably the same exact size*) with a glazed coating. Most glazes, which require a second firing during their processing to seal the glazing atop the surface of the tile, are fairly impervious to water and so are suitable for wet installations. This process is more commonly used on wall tiles that are generally ¼" too ⅜" thick. The coating is usually pretty thick and slick and so it's usually not ideal for floor tiles. Floor tiles are made thicker, usually ½" to ¾", and the second firing will give them a thicker glaze. Also, many have a built-in skid-resistant or even a textured surface to make them ideal for walking on.

There are many shapes and sizes of tile available, which can be mixed to create various patterns. **Field tiles** all have one thing in common: that is, that they have no finished edge. A border can be incorporated in many ways on a floor, counter, or wall pattern. For **border tiles,** there are many choices. Which ones are incorporated depend upon taste as well as what substrate is used. Smaller tiles may also come mounted in sheets. Spaced evenly and in rows on either a fabric or paper mesh sheet, they are easy to install, provided you line up each sheet (*anywhere from 12" x 12" to 2' x 3'*) with the same amount of spacing that the individual tiles were set in the factory.

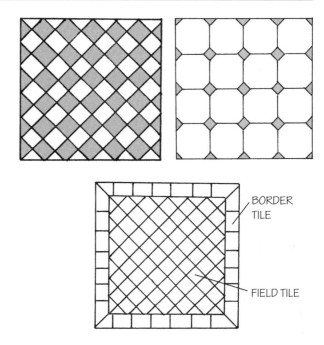

BORDER TILE

FIELD TILE

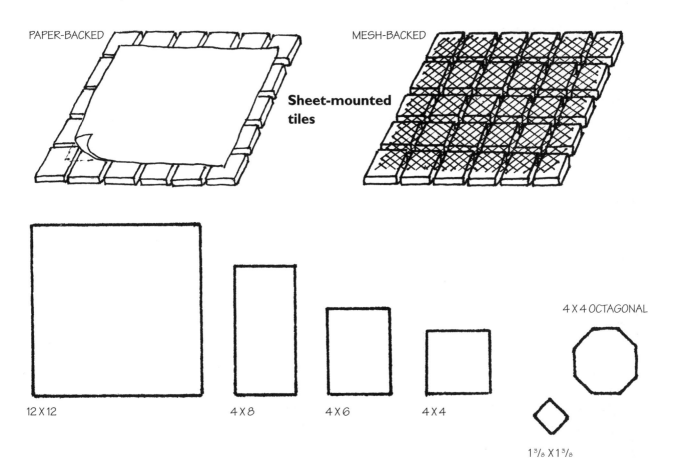

PAPER-BACKED

MESH-BACKED

Sheet-mounted tiles

12 X 12

4 X 8

4 X 6

4 X 4

4 X 4 OCTAGONAL

$1^{3}/_{8}$ X $1^{3}/_{8}$

The Voice of Experience

The human hand rarely comes into contact with a tile today, at least until it is installed. Just like the carpenters of olden days who brought their planes and saws to a job and made the moldings that they installed, the tilemakers of ancient times installed tile that they'd manufactured themselves.

Ceramic tiles are probably the most common and easily found in stores. They are available in a wide variety of sizes and colors and are manufactured for both floor and wall applications. Most have a glazed finish over a soft ceramic body that can be scored and snapped easily without a machine (*wet saw*). I'll go into that a bit more in the "Tools" section of this chapter.

Most **marbles** have a bit of a glaze coating on them and, though they are also considered a fairly soft tile (*easy to cut*), they require a wet saw to make cuts. After installation it can't hurt, either, to finish by sealing the entire surface with a water-based sealer. I'll go into that in the final chapter. A **granite** is a very dense and hard-bodied tile. The last floor we did with granite required multiple cuts, so I rented a wet saw for that job only, to avoid putting too much stress on my own saw, its blade, and the machinery.

I am partial to irregular slate patterns and colors. These and other thicker tiles designated for exterior use generally fall into the category of unglazed **quarry tiles.** Commonly found on patios and sidewalks, these tiles have gained popularity for indoor use, especially in the past twenty years, because of their "raw" and "natural" look. When you buy a bunch of these for an installation no two tiles are exactly alike and the thicknesses vary. They generally come unsealed, and that step would have to be done during the installation.

Cement-bodied tiles, also used originally outdoors, can also have a beautiful and "natural" unprocessed look. **Saltillo tile** (*named after the town in Mexico where they're made*) is a prime example of this: the commonly found 12" x 12" tiles are still made in accordance with the age-old tradition of mixing the cement, sand, and water and either pouring it into molds or rolling and pressing it into wood boxes for their shape. Though many travel through the kiln, most still begin their curing process by being left in the sun for baking, as the tradesman tends to other aspects of his/her farm. Evidence of this is apparent; because if you look closely you may very well find one with a little chicken footprint on it!

The Voice of Experience

The "veins" that run through marble are certainly among the attributes that give it such identifiable and wondrous beauty. Still, be careful and check each tile when you go with marble. A vein that runs from one end of the tile to the other, or through the thickness (*from the surface to the back*), or worse, both, usually indicates a weak spot on the tile. It may break very easily and really isn't advisable to be used on a floor.

Besides the bill of sale, it's always a good idea to save a couple of extra whole tiles. Up until the sixties most tiles were stamped on the back with the manufacturer's name as well as the specific tile's identification number. Today many still are, and that comes in handy should you ever have to replace a few damaged ones.

Tools of the Trade

Floats and Trowels

The basic and most recognized tools of the tiler are the **floats** and **trowels.** The **wood float** is used mostly for installing a mortar bed. It is not costly (*about $6*) and can come in handy for various duties. The **rubber float** is used to force the grout into the crevices after the tile has been set, and a decent one (*about $12*) will last you for at least a half dozen jobs. If you use a latex liquid adhesive with the grout, then the rubber's just a bit more difficult to clean than if you're using water. It's worth it, though, as the latex is only going to benefit any tiling job you do, whether it's a wet installation or not. A **margin trowel** is good for mixing as well as a poking, sliding, and tweaking the set tile, and becomes an all-around back-pocket tool. To "butter" the back of specialty tiles or tight areas, there is the gauge (**buttering**) trowel. I actually use the **gauge trowel** rarely and butter the tiles with either the margin trowel or a 3" putty knife, which I've always got in my back pocket, also. When I look at the gauge trowel I always think of my older brother, who used to be a mason and put up stone chimneys in newly constructed houses.

A **plain metal trowel** will do the job in taping back board membranes and complement the wood float for smoothing soft uneven areas in the underlayment. The **notched trowel** is used to apply the thinset to the underlay. There are two

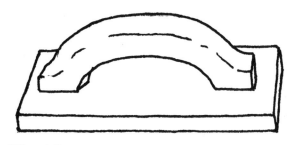

Wood float

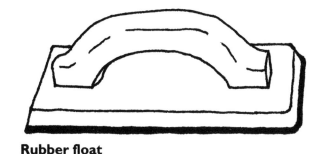

Rubber float

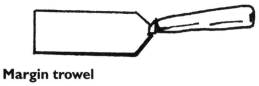

Margin trowel

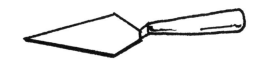

Buttering trowel

kinds of teeth: pointed and square. Generally the **pointed** are used for putting gooey adhesives down, specifically what is used for linoleum and prefinished wood flooring, or if doing a traditional mortar bed in a wet installation, spreading out the black asphalt gum. The **squared-teeth trowels** are used primarily for spreading the sandy adhesives down: specifically thinset. They're available in a smaller ¼" or ³/₁₆", or the larger ½"—even ½" wide teeth by ¾". A larger tooth would give you a thicker thinset bed. Which one you would use would depend upon the size of the tile and where it would be applied. A 12" x 12" tile set in an entryway would work well with the mortar spread out with a ½" toothed trowel, for instance.

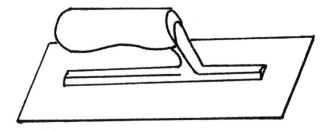

Plain metal trowel

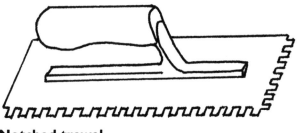

Notched trowel

Measuring and Marking Tools

Once the substrate or underlayment is ready, whether the flat concrete floor has been "primed," a mud layer has been floated, or the backer board has been installed, you'll want to do a bit of layout on the floor. Besides having a **retractable** (*at least 25' long*) **tape measure,** a large **carpenter's square,** and a 36" or 48" **straightedge** will provide immeasurable help throughout the job: planning and sketching the layout, and cutting the tiles themselves. Though it generally takes a helper to snap one, a **chalk line** will aid in getting long, dependably straight lines on your underlayment for plotting out where the tiles will go.

Depending upon the extent of the job and the area you'll be tiling, **levels** will come into play. If you are not going to make your own mud and put down a mortar bed, then you probably won't need a 48" one. A floor job won't require one if the underlay is in place. For any job though,

especially walls, I generally make sure I have a **24" level** as well as a **torpedo level,** just to keep my rows accurate and plumb. We also have several straightedges handy. One is 48" and made of metal, and then I will use lengths of anywhere from 12" to 36" made of a sturdy wood from a recent job. They aid in the layout and also help you keep your rows of tile aligned. Pine is okay, though a 1" x 2" or 1" x 4" piece of poplar would be better because it's a bit harder and less likely to warp when wet. And one or two of these strips will also become an essential tool in the layout portion of the job. Marked with your specific tile width and grout spacing and usually made of a straight piece of 1" x 2", it is called a **jury stick.** I'll describe this more in detail in the "Layout" section of this chapter.

When measuring the tiles for the cuts that'll be required on trim pieces, you obviously want the mark to stay on the surface while cutting.

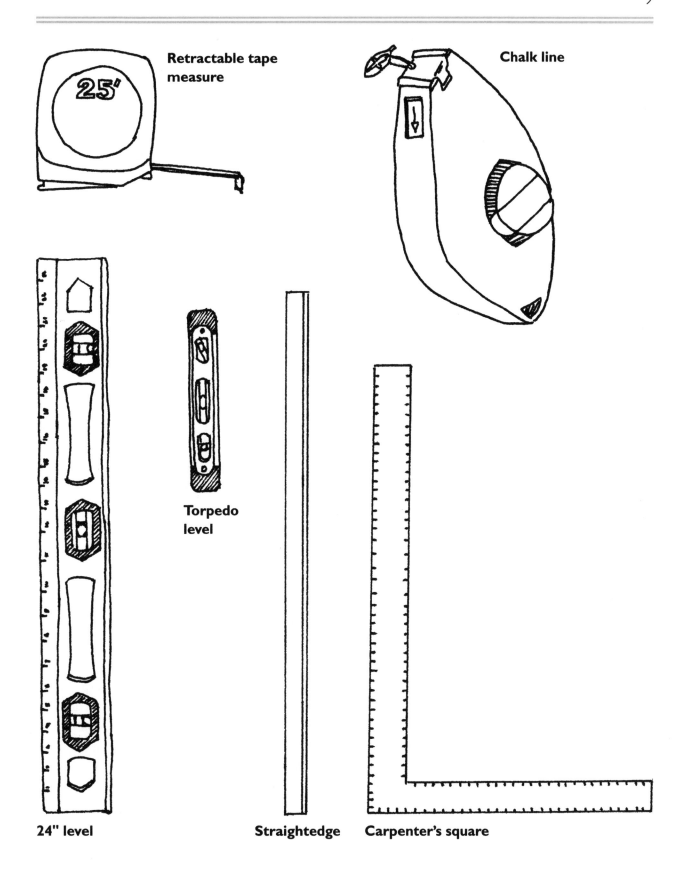

Retractable tape measure

Chalk line

Torpedo level

24" level

Straightedge

Carpenter's square

The water coming off the blade when a wet saw is on will wash off some things and leave others.

A **china marker** will leave a clear mark on most tiles, especially granite or marble. It can be wiped off easily before you grout and place the tiles. I also use a **pencil** on slates and natural tiles as the point makes a clearer mark than a china marker does on the rough surface. And I always keep a **permanent marker** around for when we are working with a wet saw and need to make intricate marks on smooth ceramic tile surfaces, like a curve around a bath fixture, for instance. The "permanent" ink will hold up longer under the water as you make the runs back and forth with the blade, certainly longer than a pencil or china marker would. Any mark left can easily be wiped off when the tile is set in place. When making curved or intricate cuts under the wet saw, you'll have the best bet holding your mark by covering the top surface of the dry tile with **blue painter's tape** and making the mark on the tape with the permanent marker. Then once the cut is made the excess tape can be taken off and thrown away.

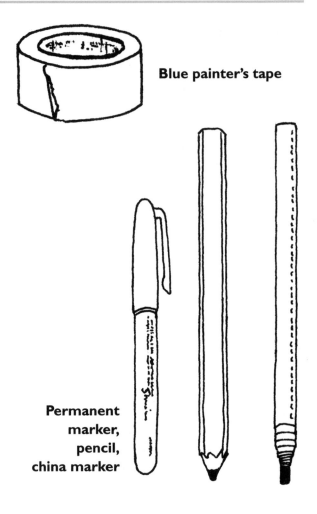

Blue painter's tape

Permanent marker, pencil, china marker

Your Toolbox Stuff

When working tile onto a surface, it'll become obvious once you start that not all the tiles will be whole going down. The field tile generally will, but when coming to an edge (*ceiling, floor, backsplash, or corner of a wall*) your tile will require cuts to fit in place and complete the surface. Those cut edges will most certainly be rougher than the natural (*or machine*) edge, especially with any ceramic tile. Having a **stone** on hand always helps. You can give that edge a little smoothing/sanding by rubbing it back and forth a few times on the stone. It is generally less dense than a chisel honing stone.

There are a few miscellaneous plumbing tools that I keep on hand when we are called upon to hookup or unhook bath and kitchen fixtures, like the **crescent wrench, monkey wrench, pry bar,** and **Teflon tape.**

A **staple gun** will be used if a waterproofing membrane is installed (*see later in this chapter*). We don't need them or use them when doing simple entryway or other non-wet installations, but one is generally in the toolbox, anyway.

I have a plastic toolbox to carry some of my stuff, but I usually like to cart most of my tools and needed accessories in **5-gallon buckets.** I have

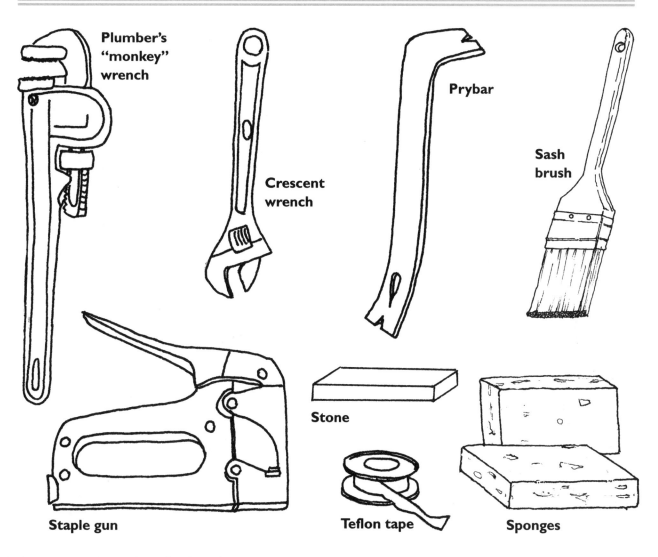

Plumber's "monkey" wrench

Crescent wrench

Prybar

Sash brush

Staple gun

Stone

Teflon tape

Sponges

three—I got them after I finished the material that had been in them: joint compound is the most likely source. They are useful for mixing thinset and grout, holding the water and sponges for the continual wiping/cleaning that'll be called for, and (*should you be going the route of putting down a mortar bed*) measuring out for mud mix. These buckets (empty) can be purchased for about $4 or $5 apiece at a home improvement store.

Along with the bucket comes the large **sponge.** It ought to be absorbent, and the more the merrier, as you will use one for cleaning-as-you-go when putting the mortar adhesive down

and several clean ones when grouting. As much as I am a naturalist, I must note that the "natural" ones are just terrible—the best are the simple large yellow cellulose ones that seem to hold a lot of water. They cost $2 or $3 apiece, and you ought to buy at least three. That's for the wet-wiping. Have as many clean absorbent **white rags** around as you can. With them you can wipe the tile facing dry each time the grout is sealed at the very end. And, of course, for sealing the grout, you need a good-quality 2" or 2½" **sash brush** made of tynex or polyester fibers.

Though more an accessory than an actual tool, the **spacers** and **wedges** are necessary for wall installations. Placed between the tiles in the corners and/or along the sides as they are set in the thinset, they are helpful with factory-made tiles (*all uniformly the same size*) but aren't as good when used uniformly with slates and other natural tiles. They come in variety of sizes, starting with the smallest, $^1/_{16}$", and going up to the huge $^1/_4$" for a large grouting space. The ones made of rubber are the best to use: they are the most pliable and, because they are removed before the grouting, they can pretty much be reused. They also come in hard plastic, but those are not easy to work with, though we have used them in a pinch. We also cut up a whole bunch of little cardboard squares and keep them on hand if we are working with a natural tile on the wall. They help in conjunction with the spacers and wedges.

A **rubber mallet,** used with a scrap piece of board called a **beating block,** will enable you to "bed" the tiles so that the surface of each area you complete is nice and flush. Have a **claw hammer** and a **cold chisel,** both of which are useful for many things, especially for removing doors for a floor tile job. Many tilers will do intricate cuts around the bottom of a door casing when installing a floor tile. However a reversible **flush-cut saw** will enable you to avoid these contoured cuts by trimming the bottom of the casing during the layout phase of the job. By allowing the tile in its thinset bed to sit *under* the molding, you will lend a cleaner look visually.

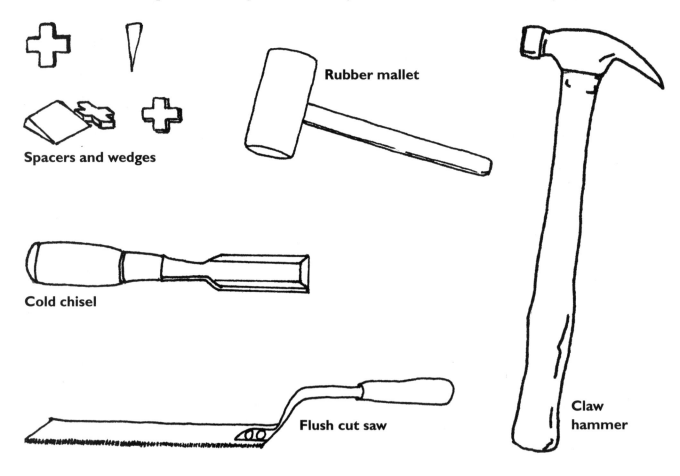

Spacers and wedges

Rubber mallet

Cold chisel

Flush cut saw

Claw hammer

A **tool belt** is not necessary, as each stage of the job seems to require few small tools—but it can't hurt. It's somewhere to put the **biters** as well as the **utility knife.** You can use a utility knife to score/cut backer board although you'll have to change the blade fairly often. A **carbide scriber** works much better, and can be found at most home improvement centers that have a tile department. Just before the grouting, the spacers can come out, but may need to be removed by a **metal pick.** Any tool with a pointed edge will do . . . something similar to but thicker than a dentist's pick. I actually use a nut pick that we

used to have in the nut bowl on the Thanksgiving table back in New Hampshire. A **caulking gun** will be used during the setting of the underlayment as well as often in the finishing portion of any job. Tilesetters who also do "light" plumbing (*that is, they remove and install the toilets in the bath makeover*) will also have a **small hacksaw,** this one designed specifically for trimming the closet bolts once the toilet has been reset over the new floor. A clean **spray bottle** will help keep the thicker grout lines from drying too quickly for times when an installation is done during a hot, dry period.

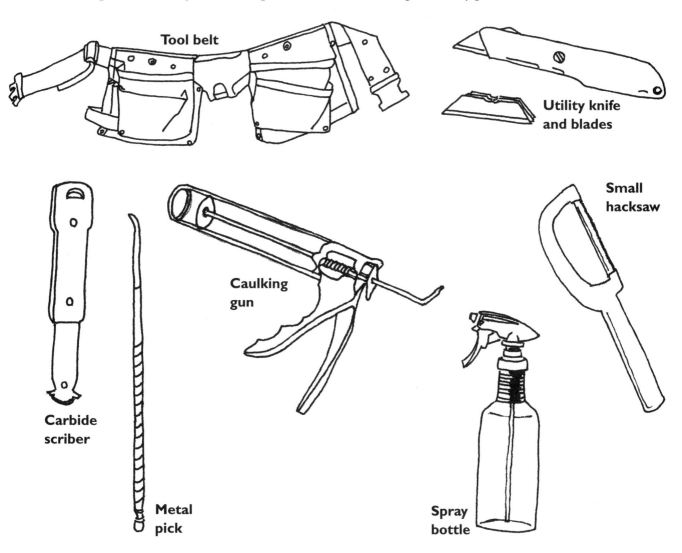

Tool belt

Utility knife and blades

Carbide scriber

Metal pick

Caulking gun

Small hacksaw

Spray bottle

Many tilers cut their backer board with a small circular saw or grinder equipped with a diamond-tipped carbide blade. But because this method raises so much dust I won't advocate it here. Backer boards can easily be cut and trimmed with a carbide scriber. However, this only works for straight cuts. If an "L" or other-than-a-straight cut is needed, we usually use the **saber saw.** And because the blades aren't that expensive I just use a regular "rough cut" blade (*if I don't have a carbide blade on hand*), which lasts for a whole job's cuts, and then I just toss it afterwards. It creates a lot less dust and airborne particles, and works just fine. Another power tool that is used regularly is the **drill.** This is used with a **Phillips head bit driver** to drive the screws into the backer board, fastening it to whatever surface it's going over. It's also used in combination with the **hole saw kit** for cutting holes in the backer board that allow the plumbing fixtures to come through, such as on the bathtub walls. You can invest in a carbide, diamond-tipped set of these bore bits, but you can also get a pretty inexpensive set at a home improvement store (*for about $15*) and they'll last for several jobs.

Worm drive circular saw

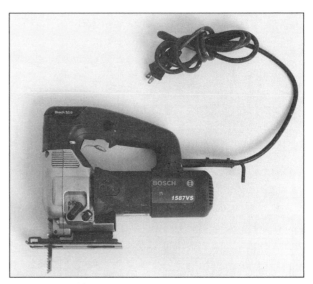

Saber saw

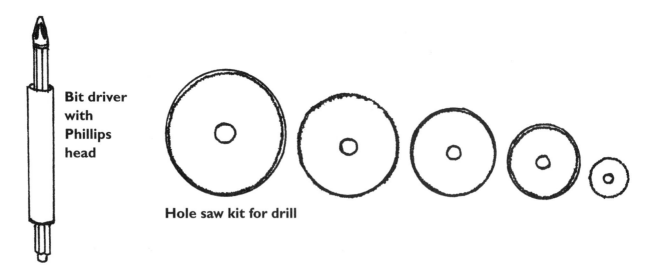

Bit driver with Phillips head

Hole saw kit for drill

The Voice of Experience

A POWER TOOL THAT GETS USED OFTEN (*though not for actually setting the tile*). If a door opens into your soon-to-be-tiled area, then chances are that door will have to be trimmed (*ripped*) at the bottom to accommodate the new height of the floor. We use a **worm-drive (hypoid) saw,** although a 7¼" **circular saw** will do the trick nicely. Figure the amount that will have to be ripped off, taking into consideration the space between the bottom of the door and the floor presently, along with the height that the new tile, thinset (¹/₈" to ¹/₄"), and underlayment will add. Remove the door at the hinges with the cold chisel and hammer, set the door on a table, sawhorses, or worktable, and mark where the new cut will be. Put two strips of blue tape on the door along the line to protect the door from the underside of the saw's guide. After you shave the bottom off, pull the tape off *toward* the bottom of the door—this will help you to avoid lifting paint off along with the tape.

Remove the door hinge pins with the cold chisel and hammer

Use the blue painter's tape to mark the amount needed to adjust the door length and "rip" the bottom of the door with the circular saw

And for Cutting the Tile

A **snap cutter** is a manual (*nonelectric*) tool that has a rubber or foam bed on which you lay the tile. By placing it against its fence, perpendicular to a center "breaking" bar, you determine where the cut will go, pull the handle with the tiny diamond-tipped scoring blade back once, and it scores the surface of the tile. By pushing back the handle once over the tile, the wings of the handle will "snap" the tile across the breaking bar (directly under the scored line). It works great for straight cuts on ceramic tile. It won't work with more complicated cuts, like an "L"-shaped one, for instance. And the cut edge is somewhat rough and thus usually requires a light sanding on the stone.

Tile biters look like pliers and have two sharp blades that pince together and do just that to

Snap cutter

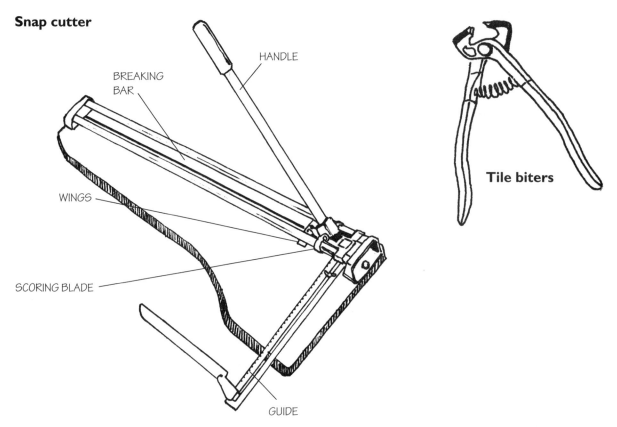

HANDLE

BREAKING BAR

WINGS

SCORING BLADE

GUIDE

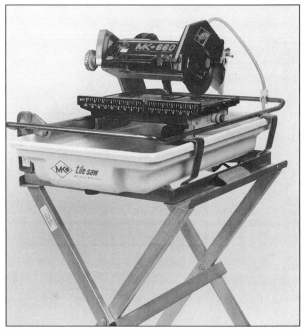

Tile biters

the tile: nip or bite away a small bit at a time. They work great with ceramic tile but are generally unsuccessful in "biting" any portion of marble, slate, or granite *(which is very hard and dense)*. They also work great for snipping off a smaller portion of a tile that the snap cutter couldn't get at.

Even if the tiles can easily be cut with a snap cutter, I really like the ease and precision of the **wet saw.** There are several variations of a wet saw: some with a moving arm and a stationary table, others with a stationary arm and a moving table. Mine has an arm equipped with the blade that moves up and down with a moving table. When in use, water is continually pumped (*from an attached filled tray below*) onto the circular blade, which spins but remains in the stationary motor

Wet saw and stand

The Voice of Experience

ONCE BITTEN . . . If the straight portion of a tile that needs to be cut is too small for the snap cutter, you can do it with the biters. First score the line of waste, either with the snap cutter blade or the end of the carbide scriber. Start by putting the jaws just halfway onto the tile along the line, holding the underside at a slight angle. By attempting the first bite with a portion of the jaws, you can avoid taking off tile beyond the waste portion (*and into the part that you'll need*). Once bitten there, bite off the other end of the line in the same way. Finish by biting the remainder of the waste, again with the biters at a slight angle. If there is excess tile along your line, finish biting it off and then run it over the stone. For curved cuts, go in to the marked waste portion a nibble at a time, starting away from the mark and moving toward it.

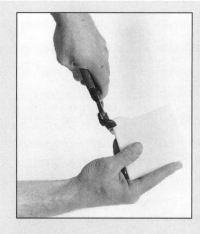

Begin biting one end of the scored area

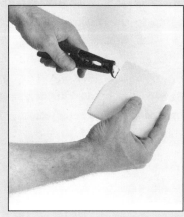

Before coming to the end, bite off the other end, to avoid a crooked bite

housing. It can be set on the floor but is obviously easier on a worktable or stand. Most saws come with one that locks snugly under the saw.

You can get an excellent industrial 2 hp (*horsepower*) wet saw for around $900 that has a 10" blade and sliding table that can accommodate 18" tiles and make 12" diagonal cuts. A saw this size is what many tilers in the industry use, and it weighs about 110 pounds. The one I've been using for the past six years is moderately lightweight with ¾ hp and a 7" blade. I got it for $550, along with a heavy-duty metal stand for another $80. It will cut large 15" x 15" tiles with

ease, and 12" x 12" tiles on the diagonal with a bit of maneuvering. I just saw a cute little saw made by the same company that makes mine, selling for under $200. It has a sliding table and claims to cut tile sizes up to 14" and 10" on the diagonal, which is pretty good. Online I came across the same size saw, weighing just under 40 pounds and selling for $299 from a very reputable power tool company. There was even a small wet saw offered through this online tool seller that had ⅓ hp and cost $70. It looks like a little table saw where the blade comes up through the stationary table and the tile itself

The Voice of Experience

If you decide to buy a wet saw, read through the directions carefully before you use it. A common problem that often comes up: the water may not be pumping water onto the blade, which is the essential key to making the cuts. Check the pump; it may have rolled onto its side in the tray and therefore not in position to do its job. Or there may be air or dust clogging the passage from the pump to the motor. You can almost always remedy the situation by pulling the little hose off the end of the motor and blowing into it, both the motor end and then through the hose toward the pump. When it's reattached, try the motor again and see if water sprays through this time.

The Voice of Experience

Be certain that once the motor is turned on that water is spraying onto the blade before you begin to run the tile through it. If you try to cut a piece of tile with no water cooling and wetting the saw blade, you will quickly damage your $75 diamond-tipped blade. Anyway, if you do start the cut you'll see sparks fly and this should tell you that something is wrong.

must be moved to make the cut. I've never seen anything so cheap before, and since blades themselves go for anywhere between $40 and $300, I can't imagine that this is too good a deal.

A wet saw may be rented from a tool rental place for anywhere from $25 to $40 per day and the price may include a stand. It's certainly worth the rental fee if you're doing even one tile installation. Even though straight cuts can be made quickly with a snap cutter, you're restricted as to how small a piece can be cut by one, and, as I said earlier, you can't made odd-shaped cuts. And you're also restricted in what kind of tile you can use—a snap cutter will not successfully score a piece of marble or slate for a cut. The wet saw makes smooth, straight cuts through ceramic, marble, slate, and granite. You can get a rounded

edge with marble or granite with multiple cuts from several angles.

Because of the spray of water and the wet tile shavings they throw off, wet saws are best set up outside. Often we've done tile jobs in apartments where this just wasn't possible. Set down a 9' x 12' thick piece of plastic (*at least 3 mil*) and then set the saw in the center of it—you should be okay. Lay cloth drop cloths from the tile saw along the route to the tile area. While making your cuts, periodically sop up any puddles collecting underneath the saw with your sponge. Lastly, it is imperative that the saw be plugged into a grounded outlet receptacle for use.

✐ The Wet Stuff: Latex Additives, Thinset, Grouts, Sealants, Caulks

A CERTAIN WHITE LIQUIDY MATERIAL HAS really gained popularity in the last fifteen years and has become essential for most tilesetters. Most commonly called a **latex additive,** it was introduced as a substitute mixing element for water in mixing up sand and cement for a mortar bed. It then was used, again as a substitute for water, when mixing grout, first in wet installations only, and now it is used pretty much in place of water for all tile installations. Even if the **thinset** or **grout** specifies that a "bonding additive" has been added to the powdered mix, it will only make your installation stronger to use the additive in place of water. It may also be called liquid adhesive and can be used to prime surfaces that are dry and would otherwise draw too much moisture from your thinset mixture (*concrete*) or to give the surface a nice bonding agent that was originally something other than a tile substrate (*like linoleum or a painted wall*).

Adhesives

Adhesives, or mastics, refer to a material that is used to "glue" something down, and they come in organic and cement-based varieties. The organic mastics come both solvent and water-based and are generally the choice of do-it-yourselfers, because they come premixed. They tend to not be as strong as the cement-based adhesives, and also are limited to be used on only smooth, sealed tiles, because the excess is difficult to clean off when applying. The cement-based adhesive refers to **thick-bed** (*mortar or mud, which I'll go into later in this chapter*)

and the **thinsets,** which are the adhesives of choice for most tradesmen.

Thinset can be ready-mixed, also, although the adhesives in the powder form are preferred for most jobs, as the tiler has more control over the thickness and drying time. There are both latex (*water-based*) and petroleum products available. For Tiling 101 here we'll stick with the latex products for use. If you do decide to use a petroleum-based grout, be sure to check the

The Voice of Experience

JUST LIKE MAKING BREAD. I never was much of a cook, and though I've baked from time to time, I've pretty much become a eat-whatever-takes-the-least-amount-of-time-to-prepare kind of guy. But when I was growing up we would visit my grandmother in Massachusetts and whenever she asked my brothers and I to help her make bread (*from scratch*) we happily agreed. Gram would guide me in mixing the flour with the liquid ingredients to get just the right consistency. It seemed to require strong forearms and triceps and yet Gram (*who was in her seventies and I don't think ever did any weightlifting at the gym*) showed us that it was really a cathartic and enjoyable experience. Today, every time I mix a batch of thinset or grout with a margin trowel in a bucket, I realize how close the two arts actually are. Too runny? Sprinkle on more flour (*grout*). Too thick? Add more water (*liquid additive*).

manufacturer's instructions, and be sure that it's compatible with the underlayment.

Mixing is pretty straight-forward—double-check the product's directions for any special instructions. I usually use a nice big 5-gallon bucket. Don a pair of latex gloves and pour a good amount into the bucket. Mix in the liquid additive or water, a bit at a time, with the margin trowel. Be careful to get all the dry mixed in by scraping the bottom and sides of the container as you continue to fold in the additive. A nice consistency is reached when the trowel stands up in the mixture and starts to lean only slightly.

I have an 18" paddle that, when used with my ½" drill, I can mix both thinset and grout quickly. It really comes in handy when you are doing big jobs. I didn't use one for the first few bathrooms or kitchen counters I did, and I don't think it's a must-use tool. It will save time, but you can get the same results with the margin trowel.

Mixing paddle

You can take an amount out of the bucket with the flat side of the toothed trowel and dollop it inside the square (*marked on the underlayment*) that you're starting on. Or plop some down with the margin trowel. I usually keep the margin trowel handy, as well as a 3" putty knife in my back pocket or tool belt, to help the stuff behave. First use the flat edge of the trowel and spread the thinset evenly within the starting square. Then, holding the toothed edge at a consistent angle to the surface (*the angle will depend upon how high you want the bed to sit*), swipe and drag it across the layer of thinset to get a nice

bed. The reason you spread it like this is to get the best possible bond to the substrate (*underlayment*), whatever you are using. If you only tooth-troweled the bed in place, you can actually decrease the strength of the bond by 50%

Spread the thinset first with the flat side of the trowel

Then use the toothed side of the trowel to create the thinset bed

Whether doing a wall, floor, or counter, take your time. Work within the grids that you pre-drew with pencil and chalk over the underlayment. Set the tiles in place, pushing in the spacers as you go along. Although you want to avoid moving them too much once placed in the bed, you've got a little time to adjust them as you go along. A straightedge can be used as well as your jury stick to continually align the tiles and make sure that you're keeping nice and straight and within the proposed pattern. As you move along setting the tiles and have made any slight adjustment, tap them into place with the beating block and rubber mallet. If a tile looks a bit low in one place, your bed may be a little thin there: pick it up and apply some thinset directly to the back of the tile with the buttering trowel. This is called (*can you guess?*) "buttering" the piece, and you can also use the margin trowel to get a little extra build-up under one tile. When I'm doing specially cut pieces that go around a toilet flange, shower fixtures, or border tiles, I generally don't extend the bed to where the tile will go, and I butter each piece individually to set it.

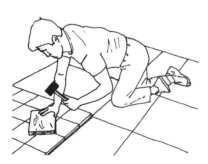

As you set the tiles, move the beating block over them, tapping them into place

"Buttering" the back of the tile with the buttering trowel

The Voice of Experience

JUST RIGHT. To test whether the consistency of the thinset is good for your tile, set one into the bed. Pull it up and check the tile: if it only partially covered the backside, it's probably too dry; also, the bed may not be thick enough. If the toothed bed seems to sink down even before you set the tile, it may be too runny. Either way you won't get a good bond for your tile. If the tile sits nicely in the bed and then pulls away with difficulty and is covered entirely on the backside, then you're on the money with your consistency.

Pick up the tile to check for coverage: tile pictured here not adequately covered, thinset too dry

Cleanup

Day-old dried thinset (*found on top of the tiles or popping out from between them*) can be scraped off. Beyond that it gets substantially harder and, within a week or so, it's almost impossible to get rid of it. Most tilers do the cleanup the next day, after the tiles are all set, and when they're removing the spacers. I usually keep a separate bucket of warm water and a sponge and clean up as I install . . . it's easier for me to keep things organized in my mind and I think I save time. Either way works, though. Also, the unused thinset should be scraped out of the bucket and put in the trash, not *ever* in the toilet or sink. Even the residue as it is cleaned on the inside surface of the bucket ought to get dumped out in the yard somewhere, maybe on some rocks, and then rinsed with the hose. If that option isn't available, be sure to dilute the trace amounts left in the container as you wipe it clean and then flush it down the toilet (*we're talking about the residue, only, here*) and then a follow-up flush.

Grout

Grouts come in **sanded** and un- or **nonsanded** mixtures. They are both mixed and applied the same way, but the consistency is different for the obvious reason: the nonsanded is creamier and smooth and the sanded has sand mixed in with it and so has a more "sandy" feel to it. Although mixing them with a liquid additive will enable both to be strong and resistant to cracking, the nonsanded is designed for tile spacing of up to $^1/_{16}$". The sanded should be used for gaps wider than that: ⅛", ¼", and ⅜". The size of the grain in the sand ought to be bigger for the larger spaces . . . check the specifications on the bag

when you buy the product to be sure that your spacing and choice of grout correlate.

Mixing it successfully is similar to getting a batch of thinset ready. Use a 5-gallon bucket and margin trowel and slowly add the liquid additive. Oh, and don your latex or rubber gloves now too, as this stuff is not only difficult to get out of the pores of your skin but it'll really dry your hands out as well. Also, set aside a separate 5-gallon bucket of water with a couple of sponges. If you've got a paddle for the drill, great: blend away, occasionally scraping the bottom and sides of the bucket with the trowel to be sure all the dry ingredients are in the mix. Take care not too add too much, as just a small amount will make the grout soupy. The consistency for the grout that you're looking for is a bit softer than the thinset. The margin trowel shouldn't really stand up in the mix; it ought to slowly sink. With latex products (*which is what we're using in this book*), mix thoroughly and then let sit for a few minutes (*check the mixing directions of this particular product for the suggested amount of time*). This period is called slaking. Once passed, the grout will seem to have hardened substantially, but turn it over a few times with the margin trowel and it will regain its soft, puttylike consistency.

Working with grout is a bit different than working with thinset . . . it's almost an art form, really: a bit tricky, but enjoyable to be sure. First thing, wet the top surface of the tiles in the area that you plan to start, either with the sponge or the spray bottle. (*All tiles are absorbent, even glazed ceramic ones, and will usurp the moisture out of the grout as you try to work it into the joints.*) Use the rubber float to get a big gob out of the bucket (*or use the margin trowel*) and plop it on the area where you plan to begin. Work the grout into the joints, pushing the float in different directions over the tiles. Drag the surplus grout on the tiles along with the float as you expand your area. Now, I will generally work in a 3' x 4' square before I go back and begin wiping off the excess on the surface of the tiles. If the tile is porous or unsealed, then I might not even do this much before cleaning, and if the tile surface is smooth and glazed ceramic and the grout spacing is small, then I might do a larger area before stopping to clean.

After about 5 or 10 minutes, begin to clean the tile by wiping the surface with the wet sponges. The sponges will have to be continually rinsed out, as you'll find out soon enough . . . if you've got a partner to keep supplying you with clean sponges, the job will go so much faster. The sooner you wipe after the grout has been put in and let to set, the deeper the indent at the spacing, and, likewise, the longer you wait, the

Wipe the excess grout off the surface of the tiles

higher the grout will be that is left in the space. This is one of those things that's your choice; it'll look better, though, to keep it consistent, whatever you choose. Wipe off enough so that it looks pretty clean, taking care not to dig out too much grout from joints. Move along the same

The Voice of Experience

Come across a loose tile while grouting? Bummer . . . but it happens. Pull it up and scrape the hardening thinset off the back as well as what's left of the bed. Mix a little bit of thinset and reset the tile back in place . . . finish with the beating block and rubber mallet. Unfortunately, you can't set and grout in the same day, as the grout will crack. Mask off the surrounding space of the tile and continue grouting the *rest* of the tiles' spacing. Let the repaired tile sit until the next day before finishing the grout around it.

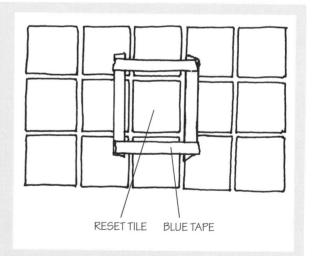

RESET TILE   BLUE TAPE

Remove the blue tape the day after and finish the grout around the reset tile.

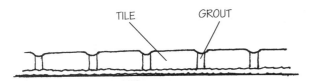

TILE   GROUT

The sooner you wash the excess grout off the surface of the tile the lower the grout level will be in the spacing between the tiles

way, doing another section. Once you've gone ahead ½ hour or so, backtrack and wipe the "haze" off the surface of the tile. Many tilers leave this on until the next day and wipe it off with a mesh cheesecloth. I find that it is so much easier to take care of it now, at this point. Also, sometimes the haze is so difficult to remove that the new surface requires an "acid wash" of muriatic acid to get it clean and ready for sealing. Besides being incredibly time-consuming and caustic on the lungs, you then have to wait another full day for the watered-down acid to dry out completely before sealing.

If you're doing a floor that has a base/border tile, or bathtub wall, or counter backsplash, you don't want to be grouting the expansion joint: I'll explain what that is right after I deal with finishing the grouting.

Cleanup

You will go through a lot of bucketfuls of water . . . continuously rinsing the sponges of the grout makes dirtied water fast. Be prepared for that, and that you'll have to get rid of it. Just like the thinset, you don't want this stuff down the sink drain. Even if you dilute it, the grain part of the grout will quickly separate and settle at the bottom of the trap under your sink—especially sanded grout. Running water won't wash it past the trap, and once it's hardened the

water flow will be permanently stemmed . . . just like a clogged heart artery. You have to figure out the best way to get rid of it. Very diluted and then dumped in a portion of the garden is a good solution. For jobs in the city, I usually flush the water in the toilet, follow with a second flush, fill up the bucket again to dilute the sediment at the bottom, stir it around, and flush again. Flush, flush, flush. It's not ideal, but toilets have a 4" waste pipe (*vs. the sink's 2" waste*) and it's pretty hard to clog them.

Sealants

The tiles and the grout have always had to be sealed, somehow, for them to repel moisture and retain their color. In olden times, one method was to seal the tiled floor with boiled linseed oil and then polish it with wax. Today most tiles are sealed in the factory and thus don't need additional sealing. The grout, however, is a different story. The grout should be sealed once it's passed a basic curing period, which is usually about 72 hours after it was installed (*check the manufacturer's directions on the product you're using*). There are both petroleum-based (*smelly*) and water-based (*latex*) products available. As always, check the manufacturer's directions on application, drying, and cleaning.

If only the grout needs sealing, I like to work with the latex products because of the low-odor and ease of application. It's pretty straightforward: pour some of the sealer into a little pan (*it's clear and has the consistency of water*) and with a 2" or 2½" sash brush liberally apply it to the grout lines. Let it absorb for a certain amount of time (*usually 15 minutes or so . . . what does your brand suggest?*) and then wipe the excess off the tile surface with a clean white rag. I usually keep two clean rags with me; one of them is the initial absorber and then I follow with the drier one. Two coats minimum is suggested . . . the second coat can usually be applied an hour or two later.

If the tile surface itself is unsealed, like many slates or natural stones, then the sooner it's done, the better. Some tilers will lay them out before the installation and seal them then. Of course you need a lot of extra space for this method. I worked with a multicolored rust-orange-brown slate in a bathroom in San Francisco once . . . it was a beautiful 8" x 8" tile: none of them were precisely the same size and they were of varying thicknesses, but that was the beauty of it, I think. It was put up on the tub walls as well as the floor. I tried to be very careful to keep the thinset off the surface while installing, and continually cleaned the fronts of the tiles as I went along. After the tiles were set but before I grouted, I put the first coat of sealer on, and it was a petroleum-based product, recommended by the merchandiser of this particular tile.

With a respirator and rubber gloves I applied it with an applicator pad and a 4" brush. I made sure the clients were not going to be around for awhile afterwards, as it was real caustic on the lungs as it dried. It was an excellent sealer, though, and once the grouting was done I finished with the same stuff and sealed the entire tiled surface including the grout.

Expansion Joints

The key to installing a tile job that will last is to make sure that the substrate or underlayment is sound. Movement causes cracks and will inevitably cause the job to fail. Since different building materials react independently to various temperatures (*movement*), an **expansion joint** is nothing more than that place where tile intersects or abuts another surface and that is left to allow for the movement: a floor to the wall or a counter unit, a counter to the backsplash, a bath wall to the tub. It is treated differently than the other spaces.

At least ¼" should be left for the inevitable contractions/expansions. Grout between the spaces of the set tiles hardens and helps form a finished bonded product, but would crack at these spots. Around plumbing fixtures on a shower wall is considered an expansion joint. The perimeter of any room, at the wall, is a place where movement will occur—where the sink sits on the tiled counter or the lip of the cooktop.

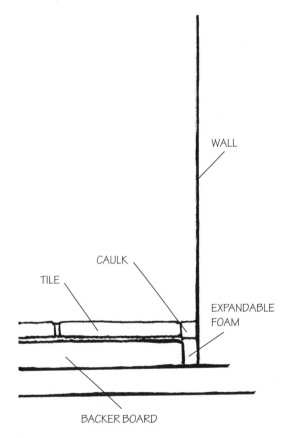

WALL

CAULK

TILE

EXPANDABLE
FOAM

BACKER BOARD

Expansion joint where the floor meets the wall

Just before the grouting is to begin, cover the expansion joint with blue painter's tape to prevent grout from getting in. After the new grout has been cleaned and sealed, slip in a small piece of expandable foam to ⅛" or so below where the top of the grout line might be. The remaining is then filled with caulking.

Caulks

There are all kinds of **caulks,** both latex- and silicone-based. Any caulk used with a tile job should have some silicone in it, even if it is a latex caulk. There is a latex version available in home improvement stores geared toward the consumer that is marketed as a "tub/tile adhesive caulk." It's pretty easy to work with, as it is water-based. The only problem is that the white one usually discolors within weeks and so looks kind of yellow. And that can be kind of cruddy when up against a white tile and/or white grout. The silicones won't discolor as quickly. Since they are solvent-based, you will need some mineral spirits to clean up and wipe off the excess.

Underlayment: Do You Need to Put a New One in? Backer Boards, Mortar Beds, Wet and Non-wet Installations, and Waterproofing Membranes

AS I SAID EARLIER, IT'S PRETTY WELL UNDERstood in the tiling industry that what you do *before* you put the actual tile down is key to whether it's going to stay down. I don't know of any tradesman (*or woman*) who would install a tile floor over floorboard planks. Everybody knows that the movement caused by the floorboards acting independently will cause the tile job to fail in no time. That's where the agreement ends among professionals. For instance, I would never install tile directly over plywood and yet I still find it suggested in tiling guides. Firstly, wood is porous and will absorb the moisture from the mastic, thus weakening it.

Before backer boards many installations consisted of going right over **plywood**. There are still old-time handymen that will swear by it as an underlayment. Why I think you're asking for trouble if you do this (*which is my second reason for not tiling directly over plywood*) is that wood will expand and contract with varying temperatures and worse, when damp (*even a hairline crack in the grout will allow moisture in and underneath the tile*) . . . and so from the get-go says, "I'm not gonna last."

Many (*if not most*) tradesmen (*and women*) that have been tiling for decades and, because of cost or habit, even look down their noses on plywood in combination with today's backer boards, will only do an installation over their own mortar bed complete with portland cement, lime, sand, and chicken wire. When I log onto INFOTILE.com's discussion groups and read some of the questions the various schools of thought are evident in the multitude of responses, from both neophytes and "experts," each convinced that theirs is the "right" way.

Most installers will say that the **thick bed installation**, or what's called a **mortar bed**, is definitely the best way to ensure that your job will be level, plumb, and sound. You have more control over the job because you're tiling over *your* substrate, vs. one that a builder put in (*and who's probably long gone, I might add*). It is considered the real tradesman-way-to-go, and requires a lot of skill and craftsmanship to execute properly. It will generally add between ½" and 1" height to the floor and consists of 30-pound felt paper stuck to the plywood subfloor with asphalt gum, 20-gauge poultry netting (*chicken wire, with 1" spacing*) stapled on top, and the cement, sand, and liquid adhesive mortar bed leveled on top of that. I will go through what it takes to mixing and installing a mortar bed a little later in this chapter for the more ambitious reader. But since this is Tile Installation 101 we'll focus on simpler methods on getting the underlayment ready for the tile.

Backer boards are most commonly found as 3' x 5' panels (*though they are made in widths up to 4' wide and lengths up to 10'*) at a home improvement supply store and various thicknesses, though ¼" (*for counters*) to ½" (*for floor and walls*) are the most common. They were introduced in the seventies and are designed to accept tile directly, thus ushering in the "thin-bed" method in a big way because of their ease of installation. The ½" ones consist of sand and cement sandwiched between fiberglass mesh, while the ¼" boards are made up of multilayered fibers of sand, minerals, and cement. Both

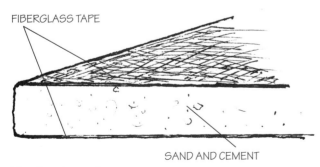

FIBERGLASS TAPE

SAND AND CEMENT

Backer board

can be cut with a trim saw, saber saw, or circular saw (*fitted with a masonry blade*), although quite a bit of fine dust becomes airborne when cut this way. Of the three saws, the saber saw usually kicks up the least amount.

Straight cuts can be done fairly easily with a carbide scriber. Several scores along the straightedge and it snaps with just a bit more effort than drywall. Once snapped at the score, then by running the scriber up and down the separation line on the other side of the piece, it can be separated into two pieces nicely. Backer boards can be screwed directly into the wall studs or plywood subfloor with drywall screws. Many installers actually use these. But because of their light weight they will tend to break off at times, so we generally use 9" x 1⅝" or 1¼" "rock" screws (*specifically made for backer boards*). It's important to be sure that the screws are countersunk so that the surface of the installed backer board doesn't have any bumps to interfere with the tile installation. I generally make pilot holes for each screw . . . this will give the screw a head start going through the cementous board and thus more likely allow you to countersink the head.

The seams can then be taped with a fiberglass joint tape and a fine-grain cement or thinset. As in all tiling ingredients, check to be sure the product you find is consistent with the thinset you plan to use and with the tile that will be used to stick it down with. As the mortar is setting I usually take my metal trowel and repeatedly spray it with water as I feather the edges of the newly taped joints so there are no bulges and bumps.

This is all well and good . . . tile is nice and waterproof, isn't it? Well, yes, at the point of installation, maybe. But all it takes is hairline cracks in the grout or expansion joints (*inevitable*) and the underlaying material as well as the building support itself (*studs, joists*) can become damaged and weakened by moisture. This is where **waterproofing membranes** come in. Although not needed for a non-wet (*or dry*) installation, they are essential to any quality tile job that's expected to last. There are many available. The least expensive is tar paper (*also tar-saturated felt paper*) and it comes in 1½' to 4'-wide-width rolls of up to 150' lengths. It can be stapled or nailed directly onto the studs and serve as a nice membrane over which the backer board can be fastened. Another is polyethylene sheeting. A thickness of 4 mil is recommended, if used. Again, stapled beneath the backer board, it protects the building materials beneath the surface nicely from the moisture.

An easy alternative is a sheet membrane. A 3-ply sheet of CPE (chlorinated polyethelene) 30 mil thick can be the substrate itself . . . folded and laminated to the backer board, plywood, or mortar bed with a (*latex*) thinset. Spun polyester fibers make it a nice "tooth" for the thinset bed of the new tile. This works especially well for counter- and vanity-top tile installations. Not usually found at home improvement centers (*indeed, most salespeople will send you to the paint-ing department as soon as you mention plastic sheeting*), you'll have to go to a tile supply house. Just call ahead to be sure they've got it. And it's

The Voice of Experience

Tar paper or polyethylene sheets shouldn't be used in combination with backer board for floor installations, as manufacturers specify that a backer board must be secured directly onto a plywood underlay. So if it is used, it must be put *beneath* the plywood.

The Voice of Experience

Don't cut corners (literally). . . . Cut and fold your pieces of CPE to fit first, before pulling out the thinset. You'll be happier because this part of the job will go so much smoother, as trying to cut and fit each piece into a wet bed of thinset can be messy. Fold up the paper a few inches for floor or counter backsplash. Trowel a thin layer of thinset, set the poly in its place, and then smooth it down (*get out any bubbles*) with a small straightedge 4" putty knife, or even a rigid plastic smoothing knife (*generally used for vinyl wallpapering*). Don't cut the corners: put some thinset into the folds, and smooth them in. If you have to staple them, be sure to touch a little silicone caulk over the heads of the staples.

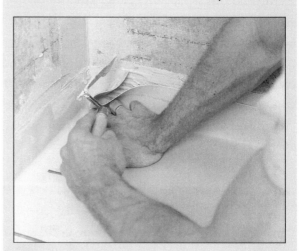

Fold, don't cut, the corners of the poly sheeting; secure the folds in with thinset

not cheap; running around $10 a linear *foot,* it is, however, well worth its weight in the role it plays in a successful waterproof tile installation.

For floors there is a new product that is gaining popularity for those who want to avoid some of the labor-intensive steps of the mortar bed (*who doesn't?*). It's called a **self-leveler cement.** It comes in 50-pound bags and works well over concrete slabs that are slightly uneven. Mixed in a concrete mixer or wheelbarrow (*if that's what is on hand*) and poured over the surface to a thickness of about ½", it levels and dries quickly. If going over plywood, staple over two sheets of a waterproofing membrane.

What Can You Tile Right Over Now?

As I stated earlier, plank floors are a no-no because of the various movements and the relative lack of support it would offer. Previously tiled floors can easily be tiled directly over, provided there are no underlying problems with the old tile job's substrate, and as long as the surface of the old tile is not too irregular a surface. Linoleum floors actually make a great underlayment if they've been put on a sound floor, i.e., a plywood or concrete subfloor (*vs. wood planks*) because they provide a nice moisture membrane. You just need to check to be sure there are no bubbles or curled edges. If there are, shave the loosed part with a utility knife and/or secure any loosened areas down, either with a staple gun or adhesive. Sand the surface first with a rough paper (*60 or so grit*) . Clean it thoroughly, make sure it's dry and apply a bonding agent—a liquid additive adhesive, preferably an epoxy-based one. If it is a wet area (*bath or kitchen floor*), then follow by sealing the staples and edges at the wall with a silicone caulk.

The Voice of Experience

There is a company that markets directly to the trade which has begun selling prefabricated corners and recessed soap dish shapes. The pieces are made of the same sand, cement, and fiberglass mesh as backer board sheets. Though more costly than building out the shapes yourself, they are certainly worth it for a beginner or a tiler in a hurry who is planning a tile install in any wet area (*bath or kitchen walls, floors, or counters*).

Drywall makes an okay surface to tile directly onto, though only for non-wet installations. If it's newly taped drywall, it should be sanded (*of course*) and primed two coats with an oil-based primer. This will create enough of a vapor barrier so that the thinset won't be in contact with the drywall surface itself. A final coat of liquid adhesive used as a sealant/primer will then make the primer ready to bond nicely with the thinset.

In this book I'm going to approach both the underlayment and the waterproofing membrane (*if one is necessary*) differently for each project, to illustrate the variety of situations you may encounter when going to tile your own area. In Chapter 1, "Installing an Entry . . . Tile," we'll put in a backer board. No waterproofing membrane necessary, as this is generally considered a non-wet installation. Chapter 2, "Installing a Bathroom Floor Tile," will need a membrane of sorts. This job has linoleum on the floor, so we'll use that as our membrane, and since it was put over a typical ¾" plywood subfloor, no additional underlayment is necessary. There's tile on the walls that needs to be changed, so in Chapter 3, "Installing Tile on Bathroom Walls," we'll remove that, install a tar paper as a waterproofing membrane directly onto the studs, and then put the ½" backer board on top. Again, in Chapter 4,

"Installing Tile on a Kitchen Counter," we'll take off whatever counter is presently sitting on the base cabinets, install a new underlayment of ¾" plywood, and then put down a sheet of polyethylene sheeting as a membrane.

The Mortar Bed: The Tradesman's Way

AS I SAID EARLIER, MANY, IF NOT MOST TILE installations will go over construction that might not be plumb, level . . . true. That, and the fact that thousands of years of history have shown just how to make a tiled area last, are the reasons why old-timers and many current professionals still like to work with the

mortar bed method—that is, mix and set in their own time-tested underlayment to accept the new tile.

This procedure, though advanced and somewhat tricky for the neophyte, can be fulfilling nevertheless. Let's figure that we'll do a bathroom floor.

FIRST THE UNDERLAY FOR THE MUD

MATERIALS CHECKLIST

- Respirator
- Long rubber gloves
- ⅛" toothed trowel
- Flat trowel
- Staple gun
- Utility knife
- Wire cutters
- 30-pound felt paper
- 1" 20-gauge poultry netting
- Asphalt gum
- 3" putty knife
- Hammer
- Margin trowel

(Not pictured here: hammer)

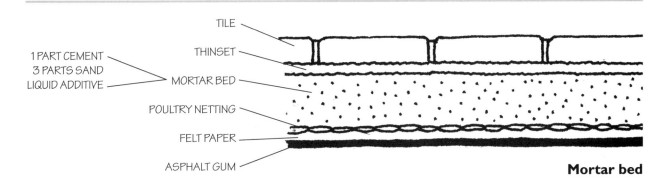

TILE
THINSET
1 PART CEMENT
3 PARTS SAND
LIQUID ADDITIVE
MORTAR BED
POULTRY NETTING
FELT PAPER
ASPHALT GUM

Mortar bed

STEP 1 GET AREA CLEAN AND SMOOTH And of course, this goes for any underlayment that would be going down. Pound down or remove any loose or protruding nails and/or remove debris (*like plaster, glue, or other blobs from construction*). If linoleum is what you're going over, cut loose any bubbles and trim the curled edges, sand it down with a rough paper, and coat it with a liquid additive (*adhesive*).

STEP 2 CUT AND FOLD THE FELT PAPER TO FIT AHEAD OF TIME. Just as in a CPE (*waterproofing membrane*), it'll make your life a lot easier if it's done now, before breaking out the smelly, messy asphalt gum. Cut it so that you

can fold/crease it at the corners and up the walls a couple of inches. Cut an "X" where the toilet flange is and press it down around it.

STEP 3 APPLY THE ASPHALT GUM TO THE FLOOR WITH THE 1/8" TOOTHED TROWEL, USING YOUR LONG RUBBER GLOVES. This stuff smells and is pretty bad on the lungs, so wear your respirator. Set the felt paper down into the asphalt bed. Smooth it out with the flat edge of a small straightedge, the margin trowel, or a 3" putty knife. Cut a few more slits at the toilet flange, stick a bit more gum beneath the flaps with the margin trowel, and set them down in place.

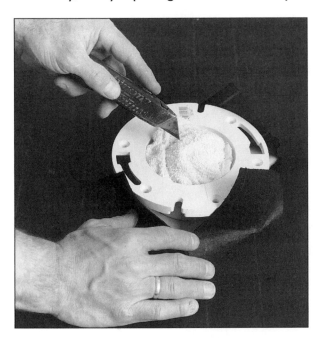

The Voice of Experience

Many, if not most, installers use the 15-pound felt paper and staple it down without the asphalt gum. However, every single one of those staples that pierces the felt paper, even though touched with butyl caulk, can become a potential problem that will allow moisture to penetrate down beyond the paper. The asphalt gum squishes in and fills the staple holes and bonds the membrane nicely to the plywood underlay.

STEP 4 CUT, FOLD, AND SET THE CHICKEN WIRE IN PLACE. Place the pieces on the floor with the curved side (*it's gonna come off a roll*) down. Keep it at least 2 inches short of the edge of the wall to allow for the expansion joint. Hold it down and staple it in place with the staple gun at least every 6 inches or so. At any seams on the field of the floor overlap at least 2 inches.

NOW FOR THE MORTAR BED

MATERIALS CHECKLIST

- Three 5-gallon buckets
- Hoe
- 3 bags sand (*with different size particles, not too fine*)
- 1 bag cement
- Liquid additive
- Water
- Wheelbarrow
- Straightedge, 48"
- Flat trowel
- Margin trowel
- Level, 24" or longer
- Several wood strips, 1" thick, of different lengths, with two at least the width of the room
- Wood float

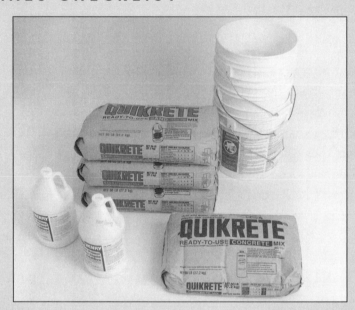

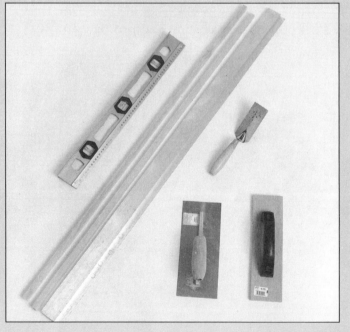

(Not pictured here: wheelbarrow, hoe)

STEP 1 WET THE SAND. Put 3 buckets of sand in the wheelbarrow and add water to it . . . just enough to dampen it. After about ¹/₂ bucket of water, you're looking for the consistency of beach sand (*the moist kind that sticks together enough to build sand castles*). **Note:** If you were making this mud mix for a wall, then you would probably want the mixture a bit moister.

STEP 2 MIX IN THE CEMENT. Spread the sand out level and pour 1 bucket of cement over the surface. Mix it together with the hoe. Take your time, and with the same motion almost as tilling a garden, "chop" the mixture through and through with the hoe, until it's nice and blended.

STEP 3 PUT IN THE LATEX ADDITIVE. Once again, level the mixture out. The best way to be sure the latex additive gets mixed thoroughly into this 4-bucketful blend is to poke

some holes (*use the handle end of the hoe or the handle of your margin trowel*) across the top and pour some additive on. Chop again, adding a little of the white liquid at a time. When it feels like a nice, moist mud ball in your hand (*not too wet*), it's ready.

STEP 4 SET UP THE AREA FOR THE MORTAR BED. Carry the stuff in a bucket to your work area. Spread a thin layer across the chicken wire. Wet two of the pieces of 1" wood (*to prevent them from warping when using them*). These are your float strips. Set them in the mud, parallel about 3¹/₂ feet apart. Make sure each is level, and then level with each other using the level.

STEP 5 POUR THE MUD BETWEEN THE FLOAT STRIPS AS WELL AS TO THE LEFT AND TO THE RIGHT OF THEM. They should be pretty secure and so won't move, but keep

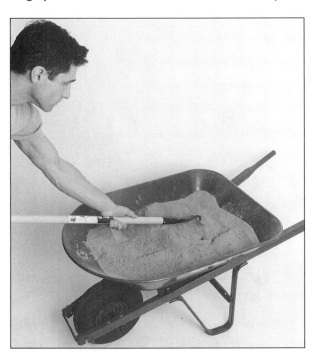

Mix the cement and sand thoroughly

Punch holes in the top of the mixture and blend in the liquid additive

checking with your level anyway. Fill the area between the strips and then pack it down firmly with the flat trowel.

Level out the float strips and put the mud between them

STEP 6 "SCREED" THE EXCESS BY DRAGGING THE 48" STRAIGHTEDGE WITH A BACK-AND-FORTH MOTION BETWEEN THE TWO FLOAT STRIPS.

STEP 7 REMOVE THE FLOAT STRIPS AND FILL IN THE CREVICES BY SPRINKLING MUD INTO THEM. Again pack it down, and now screed off the excess and make it flat by using the wood float in a circular motion. Do the same thing to any little holes or pockets that appear on your new surface. Continue around the room, using the shorter pieces of wood as float strips if need be.

Pack the mud down and then flatten the surface by screeding the excess by dragging the straightedge across, in a back-and-forth motion

Remove the float strips and fill the gaps with mud; pack with the wooden float

☞ Layout: Field Tile and Trim Tile (and More Vocabulary)

THE MAJORITY OF TILES SET ON THE FLOOR, wall, counter, or any area constitute what professionals call the **field tile.** Most of them, if not all of them, are full, uncut tiles. When the setting of the tile actually begins, these go down first. The perimeter of the area is made up of the **trim tiles.** These can be the same tile or a second tile pattern/size/color to accentuate the field. These may or may not be full tiles, depending upon the area. The trim tiles may be rough on all sides, if they are to die into a wall or backsplash, for instance. Or they could have a curved edge, also called a **bullnose** or **beveled edge,** if that edge ends on the center of a wall or floor. Whether factory-made or tailor-cut, there is a variety of ways to finish an edge.

Most tilesetters try to plan out where specifically the tiles will sit ahead, and for good reason. When you set a piece of furniture in a room you want to place it precisely so that it looks the most pleasing, don't you? Centered on a wall may or may not be the best or most obvious

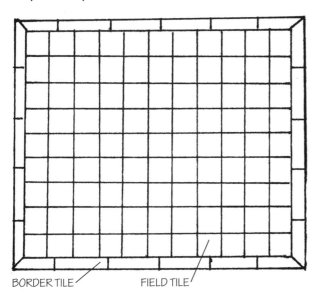

BORDER TILE   FIELD TILE

solution, but you think it out anyway, so that the chair or table looks like it "fits" in the room.

Going on this principle, when planning the layout of a floor, counter, or wall, the simplest three guides to follow are:

- **Symmetry**

- **Maximize full tiles**

- **Minimize cuts, avoid cuts that create less than half a full tile**

Whether you are doing it yourself or hiring a professional, the choices for the look on the floor, wall, or counter is very personal: they are all *yours.* If your astrological sign is Cancer (*the crab's little shell is very important to him/her and he/she takes great pain/pride/satisfaction in arranging and modifying it*), you know what I'm talking about. There is the irregularity of the various-size slate pieces to make up a mosaic, or the continual straight lines of a machine-manufactured beautiful ceramic. One tile may be the simple, elegant look for you. Or a different color, maybe even a different tile along the edge? You could throw in an accent tile throughout the area, the same size, or maybe a smaller one. Inclination could lead you to a diagonal pattern.

As you look at the room, take into consideration any doorways, what is the focal (*not necessarily the center*) point of the area, and the tile size itself. If the doorway sits smack in the center of the area then your solution would probably be to center a row of tiles down the middle of the door opening and allow the left and right flanking field tiles to be of equal proportion. Or

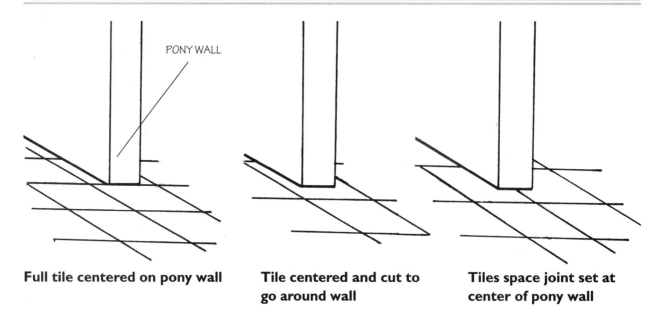

Full tile centered on pony wall   **Tile centered and cut to go around wall**   **Tiles space joint set at center of pony wall**

there may be some kind of ledge or peninsula narrow half-wall jutting out (*sometimes called a "pony" wall*) and you may want to be sure that a full tile sits at the foot of it, centered.

This naturally leads to the second tenet, which is that **you want to have as many full tiles as possible**: in other words, make the least number of cuts as possible. If you are planning a 12" x 12" granite on a countertop then any outside corners ought to be a full tile as well as any outside edges, and you'd work your way in from there. Or if that "pony" wall is narrower than your floor tile, then a full tile coming off the wall may not only balance the room but also help avoid cuts.

Most good tilers will tell you that they try to avoid setting any tiles that are less than 50% of their original size. It just doesn't look as good in an area when there is a whole row of tiles that are small slivers of the whole. Sometimes it is unavoidable, especially when symmetry is the first and foremost thing in the planning and layout. It's especially important if this is a small installation and you've got a border tile. You

would want the left side and the right side of the field tiles that are cut at the border to be as symmetrical and large as possible. But looked at in tandem, with both the balancing and trying to get as many full tiles as possible, this tenet is definitely doable. Small (*less than half-tiles*) are especially noticeable on a wall above the tub and can look a little unbalanced and cheesy.

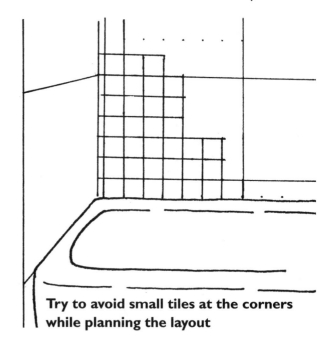

Try to avoid small tiles at the corners while planning the layout

Lay several of the tiles out in a row on the floor: place the spacers you plan to use between them. Mark a four-foot 1" x 2" with a permanent marker at each of the joints. Turn the wood over and mark the other side, maybe starting off at a halfway point this time, to give yourself a different measurement of the tiles from the end of the wood. This is called your **jury stick,** and it will help you plan the layout now, as well as keep everything in line once the installation begins. You've got a general idea of where you want the tile to start, where you want you "center" line to be. Now play with the jury stick by setting it against the wall, backsplash, or window—near the outside corners on the counter or floor, and you can hone down exactly where the rows should sit.

Make several measurements with the tape measure from each wall to determine a starting line that will be somewhat "square" in the room. No room contains perfect 90-degree angles so the multiple measurements will help you to determine what could be considered an accurate dissecting line. Make a few marks as a guide for the first line. If you don't have a partner to help you with the chalk line, then tap a nail into the underlayment at one end of the area, hook the reel onto it, uncoil the string so that it lays across the marks, and snap a line. Now take your carpenter's or try

Lay several tiles out with spacers to transfer the measurements to a jury stick

square and, again keeping in mind where your full tiles will begin, mark off the chalk line with a perpendicular line. At this point you can use the jury stick to mark boxes across the surface.

Snap a chalk line on the backer board

Use the carpenter's square and mark the center line

Now, with the jury stick, begin to mark the grids

Now you can actually lay a few rows of tile, at least to the edge (*whether it's a wall or counter backsplash*) and judge how it will look. If there is only one tile, then you can determine and go ahead and make the cuts on the border tile now.

Use the measurements on the jury stick to double-check the tiles as you set them, to be sure the tiles haven't "floated"

There are actually tilers who don't make any layout marks ahead of time . . . they just get the tile and set it, figuring and cutting along the way. They may feel that a smaller size area allows them to go by instinct, maybe.

If you approach the job with a combination of individual-piece and aesthetic planning, everything will go much smoother, and you'll be much more likely to enjoy the experience.

The Voice of Experience

WALLPAPER? Or is it tile on the wall? When I first started hanging wallcoverings 18 years ago (*I had taught myself from books*), I would cut each piece as I went along. The table would be wet from the glue and so each new piece off the dry roll would get sticky . . . the tape measure began to get traces of glue on it: the job would become more messy as I went along, and the stress level increased accordingly. Then I began cutting the long strips ahead of time and the job became more enjoyable. Another year or so passed and I decided (*before the glue was set in the tray*) just where I was going to start and took precise measurements so that I could cut each strip—long, short, or odd-shaped—ahead of time. I labeled them both on the back of the sheets and marked the wall where each piece would go. Although there were still strips that had to be recut at the last minute, I felt I was at last was able to enjoy the hanging process.

◁ Safety (and a Few More Tools)

THERE ARE SILICATES, AMONG OTHER THINGS, in mastics, cements, and grouts that irritate and dry the skin. I have a long pair of **rubber gloves** that protect my hands while grouting and prevent the muddied water from going into my gloves when I need to wring the sponges out. Even for a one-time tile job it would be good (*and your hands will thank you later*) to

have a couple of pair of **latex gloves.** We've got an endless supply of them, as they're inexpensive in quantity and I'll even use them (*if no cloth gloves are available*) when cutting backer boards which are full of lime (*another irritant to your skin*). For your knees for floor work, please invest in a pair of **knee pads** (*about $15*). Applying the mortar adhesive, setting the tile, grouting, and sealing the grout will see you on your knees a lot, on a hard surface. Essential to all tilers when making a cut is some kind of protective eyewear, like a pair of glass or plastic **goggles.** I think they're necessary even when not making a tile saw cut but only snapping a tile on the snap cutter. Your lungs are perhaps the most important health concern. Although most of the materials we'll use in the book are latex- (*not epoxy-*) based, it is good to have a respirator with clean cartridges on hand. It is needed if the mortar-bed method is the way you go . . . the initial asphalt gum that's applied as an adhesive is quite toxic. And for the sealing part of the job, some slate tile sealants are also fairly caustic.

The edges of a newly cut tile are pretty sharp, as the scratches and callouses on my—as well as my coworkers—hands can attest. It is not always feasible to wear **cloth work gloves** when working

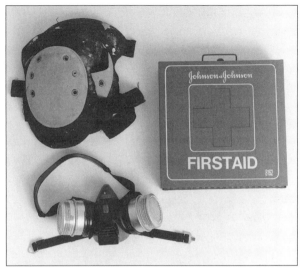

Knee pads, respirator, and first aid kit

with tiles, but having a pair on hand (*no pun intended*) wouldn't hurt. And of course we always have a stocked **first-aid kit,** full of Band-Aids, bandages, and disinfectant.

CHAPTER 1

Installing an Entry, or Main Room Floor Tile

 Assess How Much Tile You'll Need (*as Well as the Other Stuff*)

BREAKING UP THE CONTINUOUS WOOD FLOOR-ing is always nice, especially when tile is the divider. An entryway, at the front or back door, the "mudroom," a hallway, or even a main room like the dining room could be very beautiful with stone or ceramic. The measuring is pretty straightforward: use a 25' retractable tape measure and multiply the length times the width, or if your area juts out into an "L" shape be sure to include the square footage there, too. Okay; you've got your square footage. If you plan to go on a diagonal, then tell this to the merchant; he may suggest how much extra you'll need depending upon the size of the tiles. What about a border? In the same size, or perhaps a different size tile? Measure the perimeter of the room and bring this information to the store, also. How much of the border tile (*and how much less of the field tile you will need*) will all depend upon the size of each tile, and the clerk at the supply store should be able to help you out with that. Besides the tile, get the spacers, backer board, grout, thinset, and liquid additive.

 Prepare the Surface

THIS PROJECT IS THE SIMPLEST OF ALL TILE jobs because it is a dry (*non-wet*) instal-lation. There is no need for a water-proofing membrane to be installed. Still, all areas to be tiled need to be sound, and this is no different.

It must be understood that the new area is going to be higher than the adjacent floors. At the very least, the new height will be equal to the thickness of the tile itself and the thinset. If the area is currently linoleum or a concrete slab, then, with a little prep work (*as noted in the Introduction*) it can be tiled right over and the only height difference would be just that: the tile and the thinset. If the present area is covered by wood flooring, either planks or parquet, then it'll need a backer board over it. Easiest to work with is the 3' x 5'¼" backer board, and this size is readily available in most home improvement and building supply stores.

MATERIALS CHECKLIST

- Backer board: square footage = to area's
- 25' tape measure
- Straightedge, 48"
- Hammer
- Knee pads
- Drill
- Bit driver
- 1" common nails
- 1¼" screws (*for backer board*)
- Carbide scriber
- Saber saw

(Not pictured here: backer board)

First be sure that all the floorboards in the area are secure to the floor joists. The joists run perpendicular to the direction of the boards and are usually located spaced at a maximum of 16 inches apart. You can usually tell where they are by where the floor planks were nailed through when installed. Cut the backer board with the carbide scriber and straightedge by scoring it

Score the backer board where you want to cut it, using a straightedge as a guide

several times at the desired spot and then snapping it back. *(You may have to turn it over and score through the other side, because of still-attached fibers from the fiberglass mesh.)* Nail it and/or screw it onto your new area, fastening it down every 6 inches or so. Use the saber saw if necessary to cut the board to allow it to go into any doorways.

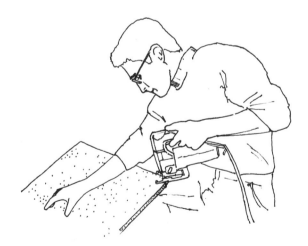

Score the backer board, flip it over, and snap it back

Cut/trim the backer board pieces to go around the doorway casings, if necessary, with the saber saw

The Voice of Experience

DOORWAY? Chances are there is a transition point somewhere, at least once, where the tile ends at a doorway. How to make it a smooth transition? A piece of molding, called a reducer, could look nice, especially if the new tile area will spill into an area with wood flooring. There are various profiles available in molding stock; just be sure that the height of the molding matches the total height of your new job: underlayment, thinset, and tile. There are also metal strips that can be used. Found in most home improvement centers in the carpeting department (*they're usually used in doorways for new carpeting*), they generally are available with brass, gold, or a silver finish.

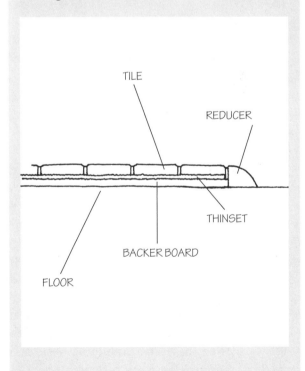

The Voice of Experience

DON'T WANT THE ADDITIONAL HEIGHT? You can *remove* the floor planking, and start at the plywood subfloor. That'll give you the height of the floor, which is going to be anywhere between 1¹/₁₆" and 1". It's a little tricky, but you can do it.

MATERIALS CHECKLIST

- ☐ Blue painter's tape
- ☐ Pencil
- ☐ Straightedge or chalk line
- ☐ Circular saw
- ☐ Chisel
- ☐ Hammer
- ☐ Goggles
- ☐ Dust mask

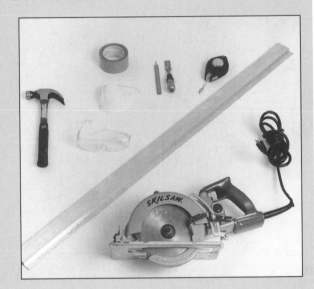

Section off the area to be cut by marking the floor with blue painter's tape. Protect the floor from the bottom of the circular saw's guide by doubling, even tripling up the tape width. Pry a floorboard up from somewhere in the center of your area with the hammer and chisel. This will allow you to see two things: what the thickness of the floor is, and whether there is indeed a plywood subfloor (*older construction homes sometimes have the finished floor planking nailed directly into the floor joists, which is one of the reasons why there is so much creaking*). If the floorboards are nailed into the joists (*there is no subfloor*), then put the piece back into place: you will have to put a backer board over the planks. Otherwise, check the thickness of the floor. Set the blade on the circular saw to that distance. (*NOTE: If you can look between the joists from the floor below— a basement, maybe—then check to see if anything has been run between them, like pipes or electrical wire/ conduit. Sometimes tradesmen have run a gas pipe inappropriately too close to the subfloor, and you want to take care when you cut if that is the case.*) Don your goggles and dust mask and turn on the saw. Bring the running blade slowly down onto the line until the saw's guide is resting flush on the floor (*be careful of kickback*). Continue around the square until you've scored the perimeter, then begin removing the floorboards. The hammer and chisel will help, especially in the corners. If the blade didn't go down far enough, extend the depth gauge

for the cut and retry . . . just be careful not to cut into the plywood subfloor (*too much*), as there could be a gas pipe running through it.

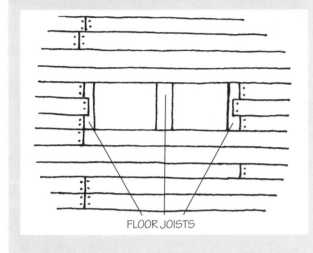

FLOOR JOISTS

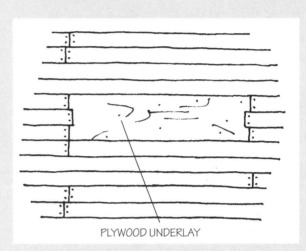

PLYWOOD UNDERLAY

⌁ Configure Your Layout

MATERIALS CHECKLIST

- Pencil, permanent marker, china marker
- Spacers
- Straightedge, 48"
- Wood strips (*for jury sticks*)
- Chalk line
- Carpenter's square

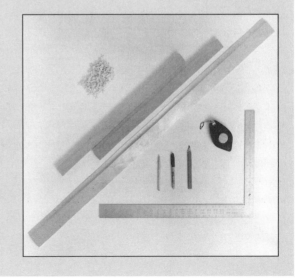

As ILLUSTRATED IN THE INTRODUCTION, DEcide the best layout for your tile. Here, we're working with one tile, a 12" x 12". The border will consist of half portions of this tile and the field tile will be full tiles, going on a diagonal. Lay out several tiles with a ¼ inch spacing and mark the jury stick. Now with the jury stick, in combination with the carpenter's square, figure where the field (*full*) tiles will be beyond the border and where the half diagonals will be.

Mark the grids with the jury stick; double-check squareness with the carpenter's square

Install the Tiles

MATERIALS CHECKLIST

- Wet saw
- Two 5-gallon buckets
- Sponge
- Toothed trowel
- Margin trowel
- Rubber mallet
- Dry thinset mix
- Spacers
- Straightedge(s)
- Beating block
- Stone

(Not pictured here: stone)

STEP 1 CUT AND MARK TILES ACCORDING TO YOUR PLANNED LAYOUT. Because of the diagonal pattern it looks like there will be some perfect half tiles (*on the diagonal*) that will sit along the border: cut those first. Be sure to run the cut edge of the diagonal tiles along the stone a few times to soften the sharp edge. Fill the wet saw's tray with water and check to be sure that the pump is working properly (*water is spraying onto the blade when the saw is turned on*). If the far right and far left end tiles need further cutting, label them on the back with the china marker. Also cut your border tiles, which will be 6" x 12", or perfect halves of the same tile.

STEP 2 MIX THE THINSET AND LET "SLAKE" (*SIT*) FOR THE RECOMMENDED TIME, ACCORDING TO THE MANUFACTURER. Then recheck the mixture: the consistency should be between cookie dough and brownie mix. Remix and you're ready to go.

The Voice of Experience

DO YOU LIVE ALONE? If so, then you're probably smart enough to realize *not* to walk on the newly laid tiles right away. Actually, stay off of them for at least a day: overnight is always good. If there is other traffic in the house it may be a good idea to set up blockades of some kind: anything to remind someone to stay off the area. I've seen all kinds of things on jobs . . . one big-time Greenwich, Connecticut, tile guy just propped up a piece of scrap drywall in the doorway of a just-set $12,000 bath.

STEP 3 SPREAD THE BED IN THE FIRST GRID. Dolloping it onto the square, first spread it with the flat edge of the toothed trowel. As I mentioned earlier, skipping this step and just spreading it with the toothed edge could weaken the bond by as much as 50%. Now comb out the bed, holding the trowel at about a 45-degree angle.

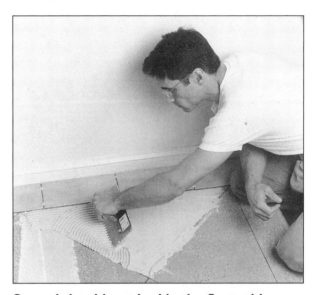

Spread the thinset bed in the first grid

STEP 4 LAY THE FIRST TILE AND THEN PICK IT UP ONCE TO CHECK THE COVERAGE. Now place four or five tiles in the bed and put in the spacers. Check the layout with the jury stick and tap/adjust them if necessary. Press them into place and tap the surface with the beating block and rubber mallet.

STEP 5 CONTINUE LAYING THE TILES. Place the field tiles and the border (*as you complete an outside edge of one side of the field*) tiles. Place, adjust, tap in with the beating block. Clean the excess thinset that squeezes up between the tiles now, as it will be a lot easier on you tomorrow when you start grouting with a "clean slate."

STEP 6 CLEAN UP . . . EMPTY THE TRAY ON THE WET SAW AND CLEAN THAT UP. If you've got access to a hose outside, that usually works pretty nicely, as all the parts showing on the motor and blade are waterproofed. If not, a nice sponge bath will do the trick. Get a clean bucket of water and place the pump in it, still plugged into the motor. Turn it on for a minute to flush it out cleanly. Scrape all the excess thin-set and throw it away in the garbage. Clean the bucket and sponges with water either by some rocks outside or flushing the diluted dirty water down the toilet, and follow with a couple of flushes to make sure it's all down.

Grout

MATERIALS CHECKLIST

- Two 5-gallon buckets
- 2 or 3 sponges
- Rubber float
- Metal pick
- Spray bottle
- White rag(s)
- Margin trowel
- Rubber or latex gloves
- Knee pads
- Dry grout
- Liquid additive

STEP 1 MIX THE GROUT IN ONE OF THE BUCKETS, DONNING YOUR GLOVES. Slowly add the liquid additive to the powder and keep turning it over with the margin trowel, being careful to get all the dry stuff on the sides and bottom of the bucket, until it's got a nice, pasty consistency. While you let it sit (*slake*) for the recommended time (*usually 15 to 20 minutes at least*), remove the spacers. It'll seem hard . . . but refold it and it should be good. If you've got to add any more additive be careful: a little goes a long way.

STEP 2 WET THE AREA AND APPLY THE GROUT. You've decided where you're going to start . . . obviously not where you'll find yourself grouted into a corner. If you have no choice and

Work the grout into the spaces with the rubber float

you have to do it that way, it's not a big deal: use your beating block or a suitable piece of wood to act as a buffer between your knees and the tile surface to avoid messing up the grout as you set it in the spaces. Working in an area that's reachable and doable in a 10-minute timespan (*usually 3' x 4' . . . less if the tile is quarry or slate*), wet down the area either with the spray bottle or a wet sponge. Plop a blob of grout onto the area and begin working it into the joints with the float, dragging the excess across the tops of the tiles as you go along.

STEP 3 CONTINUE GROUTING, AND SPONGE THE EXCESS GROUT OFF THE SURFACE OF THE TILE. Do an initial cleaning of blobs of grout left on the surface with the sponge. Avoid getting grout into the perimeter where the expansion joint will lie. Wait, though, until you've done at least two sections before backtracking and wiping/rinsing/wiping/rinsing . . . cleaning all the excess grout off the surface. As I said in the Introduction, the sooner you clean up the excess after you've pushed it into the joints, the lower the grout line level will be (*because it's wetter and will wash away easier*). If you give it a little time,

then the grout will be drier and more difficult to get off the tile, but will also leave a higher grout line. The choice is yours: just be consistent.

STEP 4 CLEAN THE GROUT "HAZE" OFF THE SURFACE OF THE TILE, USING CLEANED SPONGES AND A CLEAN WHITE RAG. This step is often left until the next day by many professionals. The longer it is left on the surface of tile, the more difficult it is to get off. If you are installing a completely smooth, glazed tile, then it will be relatively easy to wipe off later. However, if the surface is a natural (*not cement-poured, machine-processed, glazed*) it will require an "acid wash"—that is, washing and rinsing down the tiles with muriatic acid diluted in water. This requires a respirator, as it is very caustic to the skin, and then has to dry before the grout can be sealed.

The Voice of Experience

REALLY HOT, DRY CONDITIONS? If you are doing a thick spacing for your grout (*like* $^1/_4$" *or even* $^3/_8$") and the temperature is pretty high . . . and it's **dry** . . . then the grout may discolor or even crack a little while it's drying. You can protect it by spraying the new area (*focusing on the grout lines especially*) with water from a spray bottle, set on MIST. Then you can either remist the grout every few-plus hours, with less frequency as time passes, for the next 24-plus hours. Or, after the first misting, you can cover the area with Kraft or red rosin paper for the next 48 hours, letting it breathe after that for the final 24 hours before you seal the grout.

CHAPTER 2

Installing a Bathroom Floor Tile

WHERE BETTER TO HAVE TILE THAN THE bathroom? For both function and beauty, it far surpasses any other surface for the room that has the most H_2O pipes in use at any one time.

⟶ Assess How Much Tile You'll Need
(as Well as the Other Stuff)

ARMED WITH PENCIL, PAPER, AND A 25' retractable tape measure, take the square footage of the floor (*length x width*). As always, be generous (*if the length is 6' 8", consider it 7 feet, for example*). For your records take the perimeter measurement also. As I talked about in the "Underlayment" section in the Introduction: linoleum makes an excellent substrate for tile because you've got the waterproofing membrane already in place (*the linoleum!*). Besides the tile, get the backer board, grout, thinset, and liquid additive. Also, decide what size space you will want between the tiles so you can get the right size spacers and wedges.

Prepare the Surface

MATERIALS CHECKLIST

- Backer board
- 25' tape measure
- Straightedge, 48"
- Claw hammer
- Carbide scriber
- Sponge
- Saber saw
- 1⅝" screws (*for backer board*)
- Crescent wrench
- Pliers
- Hammer
- Rag
- 1" common nails
- Caulking gun
- Drill
- Toilet ring adaptor
- Silicone caulk
- 60 grit sandpaper
- Margin trowel
- Fiberglass joint tape
- 5-gallon bucket
- 2 closet bolts

(Not pictured here: backer board)

☐ Thinset

☐ Utility knife

☐ Toothed trowel

☐ Latex additive

☐ Bit driver

☐ Knee pads

STEP 1 REMOVE THE TOILET. Although relatively easy, it does take a bit of strength, as toilets weigh a lot and aren't easy to handle. Get a friend to help if you're not a bodybuilder with a good back. With the crescent wrench, unscrew the closet bolts . . . there are two, one on either side at the floor, usually hidden under pop-off caps. Turn the water off in back: the valve should go clockwise, all the way. *If you're at all hesitant at this point—perhaps the plumbing connections are*

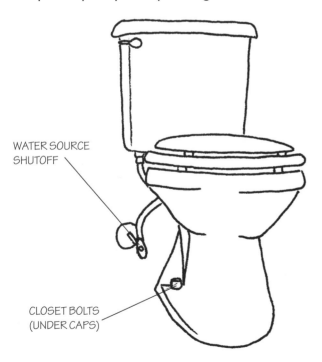

WATER SOURCE
SHUTOFF

CLOSET BOLTS
(UNDER CAPS)

very old—then by all means, call a plumber in to do it for you. With the sponge, begin transferring all the water from both the tank and the bowl into the sink, tub, or other nearby stash. Sop up every bit, as there will be less of a likelihood that something will drip when you move the toilet. Keep the rag handy and unscrew the water feel where it connects to the valve. If water is still dripping out, then tighten the valve until it stops. Carry it to a spot close by, but out of your way while you're tiling. We usually put a piece of plastic down and then cardboard, and set it atop of that. Remove the remnants of the wax ring: YUCK . . . it's gooey and usually kind of gross-looking. I try to always have on a pair of latex gloves and wipe the putty knife off pretty well when the ring is scraped entirely off. Stuff a balled-up rag into the flange opening: this will prevent gases from escaping while it is open.

STEP 2 SEAL DOWN ANY LOOSE FLAPS OF THE LINOLEUM. If there are any bubbles, then nail them down with the common nails. Rough up the surface with the 60 grit sandpaper and then clean and wipe it dry. Put a bit of the butyl or silicone caulk on any nailheads that pierced the linoleum.

STEP 3 CUT THE BACKER BOARD PAN-
ELS AHEAD TO FIT THE ROOM. As illustrated
in the Introduction, using the tape measure,
pencil, straightedge, and carbide scriber, cut the
backer board. Leave a bit of a gap at the perimeter to allow room for the expansion joint. Use
the saber saw to cut the holes for around the
toilet flange (see *illustration*).

**Trowel the thinset bed for the backer board
and "hinge" it in place**

**Use the saber saw to cut the hole in the
backer board for the toilet flange**

STEP 4 INSTALL THE BACKER BOARD
AND TAPE THE JOINTS. Mix the thinset, float
out a bed, doing each board piece a time, and
"hinge" each piece down into the bed. When
the room is finished, lay some fiberglass tape
over every joint and float the thinset over the
joints with the flat edge of the toothed trowel.
Feather the edges so that the surface is somewhat smooth. Set the closet bolts in place;
thread the bolts on top so they don't disappear
(*also this will hold them in place for now*). Don't
forget: you're making the floor higher than it

**Tape the seams with fiberglass mesh; float
the seams with thinset and the flat edge of
the toothed trowel**

was before. The toilet flange in the floor must be flush to the floor or even a bit higher to have a good seal with the bottom of the toilet, and this is where the ring adaptors come in. One should be enough, although if you're going with a thick floor tile you may need two. Seal them in place with silicone caulk.

Set the closet bolts in the toilet flange; tighten the bolts over them (*to avoid misplacing them*)

Configure Your Layout

MATERIALS CHECKLIST

- Pencil, permanent marker, china marker
- Straightedge, 48"
- Wood strip (*for jury stick*)
- Chalk line
- Carpenter's square

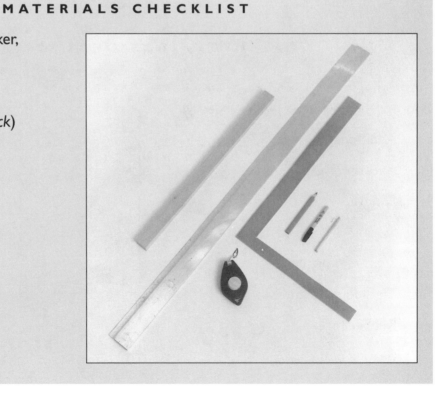

As ILLUSTRATED IN THE INTRODUCTION, decide the best layout for your tile. Here, we're working with two tiles, a 8" x 8" for the field tile and a 4" x 8" for the border tile. Lay out several field tiles with an ⅛" spacing and mark the jury stick. Now with the jury stick in combination with the carpenter's square, figure and mark where the field (*full*) tiles will be.

The Voice of Experience

Although you will need to set aside a small space for the expansion joint at the tub, figure on paying special attention to this point in both your configuration as well as the cutting/installation. In most baths, this is a very visible and sometimes focal point of the bath floor tile. So, first of all, try to avoid cuts or odd-shaped tiles along this line. And if you do have to make cuts for any of these tiles, try to make them symmetrical.

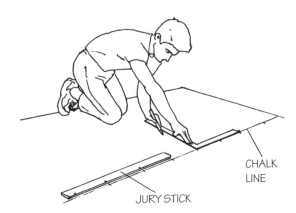

CHALK LINE

JURY STICK

Cut and Install the Tile

MATERIALS CHECKLIST

- Wet saw
- (*All materials used for the underlay*)
- Additional thinset
- Another 5-gallon bucket
- Sponge
- Stone
- Spacers, wedges
- The tile
- Rubber mallet
- Beating block
- Biters

(Not pictured here: stone)

OST OF THESE TILES WILL MOST PROBABLY
be full tiles. The ones that will be cut
here, since we're using a relatively
small tile, will have to be fairly precise (*at the
border edge, for instance*) and so it makes sense to
cut them as you install. And even though the toilet flange cuts won't need to be especially precise, it still won't matter much if we cut ahead or
when at that place and the thinset bed is set.

STEP 1 SPREAD THE BED OF THINSET
FOR THE FIRST GRID IN THE FIELD TILE.
Begin setting the tiles, first by hand, then
installing the spacers, and then use the mallet
and beating block once the tiles' spots are sure.

STEP 2 SET THE BORDER TILES AS YOU
GO ALONG BY BUTTERING THE BACK
EITHER WITH THE MARGIN TROWEL OR
THE TOOTHED TROWEL. Leave about ¼" at
the perimeter of the room for the expansion
joint. REMEMBER: "Soften (*sand*) any edges of
cut tiles with the stone before setting them in
the thinset bed.

**Back-butter the border tiles and set them
as you set the field tile**

STEP 3 FOR THE CUTS AROUND THE TOI-
LET FLANGE, MARK THE TILE. It can be run
several times under the blade of the wet saw to
get a somewhat rounded cut. Turn the tile over
and run it under the blade again, in the same
place but on the other side. The pieces can be
finished with the biters. Precision is not important because the toilet tank will sit over the hole
(*and then some*) and cover any slight irregularity.

**Mark the outline of the flange on each tile;
use blue tape to outline the waste; run it
through the wet saw for multiple cuts and
then snip off the excess with the biters**

STEP 4 FINISH SETTING THE TILES. Continue to set the sections by tiling yourself out of the room to avoid having to step on newly set tiles (in other words, don't tile yourself into a corner).

STEP 5 CLEAN UP THE WET SAW FIRST: empty its tray, then clean that up. If you have access to a hose outside, that usually works pretty nicely, as all the parts showing on the motor and blade are waterproofed. If not, a nice sponge bath will do the trick. Get a clean bucket of water and place the pump in it, still plugged into the motor. Turn it on for a minute to flush it out cleanly. Scrape all the excess thinset and throw it away in the garbage. Clean the bucket and sponges with water preferably near some rocks outside or flush the diluted dirty water down the toilet, and then follow with a couple of flushes to make sure it's all down.

Grout

MATERIALS CHECKLIST

- Two 5-gallon buckets
- 2 sponges
- Rubber float
- Metal pick
- Spray bottle
- White rag(s)
- Margin trowel
- Plumber's Teflon tape
- Crescent wrench
- Rubber or latex gloves
- Shims
- 24" level
- Small hacksaw
- Knee pads
- Grout
- Liquid additive
- Toilet wax ring

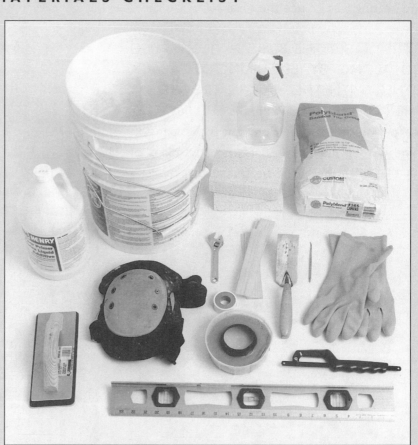

(Not pictured here: white rags)

STEP 1 REMOVE THE SPACERS. If you can't get one or two up, don't worry about it too much. As long as the spacer sits lower than where the grout line will be, it won't show afterwards.

STEP 2 MIX THE GROUT IN ONE OF THE BUCKETS, DONNING YOUR GLOVES. Slowly add the liquid additive to the powder and use the margin trowel. Let it sit (*slake*) for the recommended time (*usually 15 to 20 minutes at least*). It'll seem hard . . . but refold it and it should be fine. If you have to add any more additive, use just a *little bit*: a little goes a long way.

STEP 3 WET THE AREA AND APPLY THE GROUT. Decide where you're going to start . . . obviously not where you'll find yourself grouted into a corner. Tackle an area that's reachable and doable in a 10-minute time span (*usually 3' x 4' . . . less if the tile is quarry or slate*), wet down the area either with the spray bottle or a wet sponge. Plop a blob of grout onto the area and begin working it into the joints with the float, dragging the excess across the tops of the tiles as you go along.

STEP 4 CONTINUE GROUTING AND SPONGE THE EXCESS GROUT OFF THE SURFACE OF THE TILE. Do an initial cleaning of blobs of grout left on the surface with the sponge. Avoid getting grout into the perimeter where the expansion joint will lie. Wait, though, until you've done at least two sections before backtracking and wiping/rinsing/wiping/rinsing . . . cleaning all the excess grout off the surface. As I said in the Introduction, the sooner you clean up the excess after you've pushed it into the joints, the lower the grout line level will be (*because it's wetter and will wash away easier*). If you give it a lit-

The Voice of Experience

Clean the grout "haze" off the surface of the tile, using cleaned sponges and a clean white rag. This step is often left until the next day by many professionals. The longer it is left on the surface of the tile, the more difficult it is to get off. If you are installing a completely smooth, glazed tile, then it will be relatively easy to wipe off later. However, if the surface is a natural (*not cement-poured, machine-processed, glazed*) it will require an "acid wash"—that is, washing and rinsing down the tiles with muriatic acid diluted in water. This requires using a respirator, as the acid is very caustic to the skin, and then has to dry before the grout can be sealed.

Work the grout into the spaces; avoid the perimeter where the expansion joint is

tle time, then the grout will be drier and more difficult to get off the tile and will also leave a higher grout line. The choice is yours: just be consistent.

STEP 5 RESET THE TOILET. Okay—again you're gonna need another pair of hands. Turn the toilet on its side and press the wax ring onto the hole at the bottom. TAKE THE RAG OUT OF THE DRAIN OPENING. Take off the bolt's nuts and carry it over and carefully lower it over the flange so that the closet bolts (*already set in the floor*) come through the holes at either side of the base of the tank. Set the level on the open seat rim and adjust the tank (*only slightly at this point, as you don't want to break the seal*) down in place. Shim any edges if necessary. Once level, press down the tank, put the nuts on the ends of the closet bolts, and tighten them in place. You're now "sealing" the tank to the flange because the weight of the toilet is squishing the wax ring a bit underneath. Take care not to over-tighten the bolts. It's not too difficult to crack the tank's pedestal at this point. Once snug, cut the top of the bolts with the hacksaw. Wrap some Teflon tape around the threads of the cold water source and screw it on hand-tight, then a bit further with the crescent wrench.

Remove the rag and the nuts; push the new wax ring onto the bottom of the bowl; **NOTE:** add another ring adaptor over the flange if necessary (*to make it flush with the floor*) and seal it with silicone caulk; set the toilet over the nuts

Set the toilet in place over the flange and closet bolts. Place a level on the rim to check how it sits.

SHIM IF NECESSARY

CHAPTER 3

Installing Tile on Bathroom Walls

MEASURE FOR THE SQUARE FOOTAGE WITH a retractable tape measure, pencil, and paper. We can usually complete the walls around a normal tub with four sheets of 3' x 5' backer board (*about 60 square feet*), but

check your own space for how much you'll need. You'll need felt paper, backer board, and screws.

We're going to put a 4" x 4" ceramic tile on these walls. There are several ways to complete the edges with your new tile. Because our

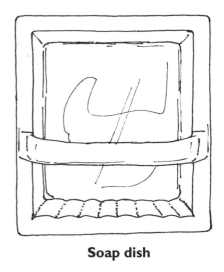

Soap dish

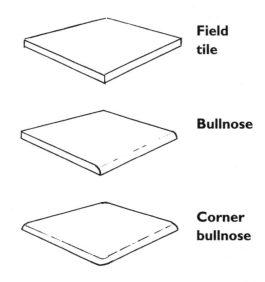

Field tile

Bullnose

Corner bullnose

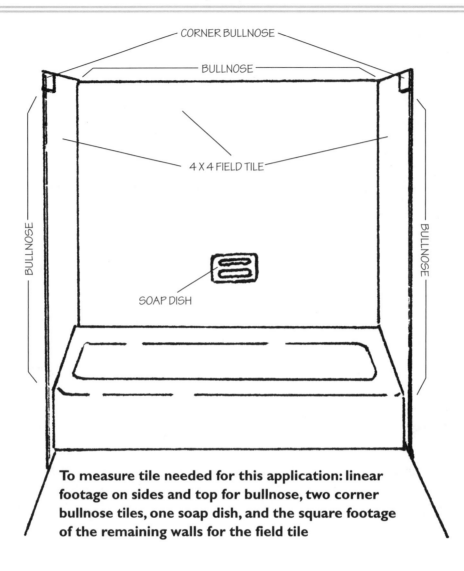

CORNER BULLNOSE

BULLNOSE

4 X 4 FIELD TILE

BULLNOSE

BULLNOSE

SOAP DISH

To measure tile needed for this application: linear footage on sides and top for bullnose, two corner bullnose tiles, one soap dish, and the square footage of the remaining walls for the field tile

underlayment is going to be at approximately the same level as the remaining (*painted*) wall, we'll use a simple bullnose tile for the sides and top edge, and a bullnose corner for the top left and right corner. So you'll need four differ-

ent tiles: the field tile, enough bullnose tiles to run along the sides and top border, two corner bullnose, and a soap dish. And don't forget the spacers, wedges, thinset, grout, and liquid additive.

Prepare the Surface

I'M GOING TO ASSUME THAT MOST OF THE READ-
ers have bathtub tiled walls already in place and want to change it . . . so we've got to

remove this old tile. Skip over this step if this isn't the case.

MATERIALS CHECKLIST

- [ ] Crescent wrench
- [ ] Hammer
- [ ] Cold chisel
- [ ] Goggles
- [ ] Blue painter's tape
- [ ] Straightedge, 48"
- [ ] Saber saw, blades
- [ ] Dust mask
- [ ] Pencil
- [ ] Boxes and thick trash bags
- [ ] Screwdriver
- [ ] Pliers
- [ ] Work gloves
- [ ] 24" level
- [ ] Utility knife
- [ ] 2" x 4"s
- [ ] Drop cloth

(Not pictured here: drop cloth or boxes)

STEP 1 REMOVE THE PLUMBING FIX-TURES. As with the toilet, if you're at all nervous about this, or your fixtures are corroded and leaky, then call a plumber and have him come and do this for you. We usually did this part ourselves, but the plumber was called in to change the "mixer" (*hot, cold, faucet pipes that sit in the wall*) and cap them once we had the old wall off, and before we put the tarpaper/backer board up. First, set a drop cloth down in the tub to help you avoid scratching it too much. *IMPORTANT: Cover the drain hole securely with blue tape so that no debris gets in.* I have come on *many* jobs that a previous workman didn't cover the drain and thus consequently the client was left with a very sluggish drain . . . it's very difficult to snake building materials out of a drainpipe, even for a plumber.

STEP 2 REMOVE THE OLD TILE AND DRY-WALL UNDERNEATH IT. This will take some banging and smashing . . . fun for a lot of people I know. Wear your goggles anyway, and use the work gloves, as most of the stuff that goes flying is sharp and/or jagged. We would fill all the old paintboxes we had and then pack the heavy-duty trash bags with the refuse. You couldn't put too much in a bag, as it is heavy stuff: we would double up the bags and still be sure not to pack in more than what would give one a backache lifting it. The tile may come off, holding onto chunks of drywall underneath. But chances are you'll have to cut a nice level line where your edge will be. Pencil it first, using the level. Then score it several times with the edge of the level and the utility knife. With some more scoring, banging, digging, you should be able to get all the old building materials away down to the studs. With the hammer, screwdriver, and pliers, remove all the nails and screws sticking out of the wall studs.

The Voice of Experience

IS ONE (*OR MORE*) OF THE STUDS ROTTED? Bummer . . . but you've got to repair it now and prevent it from continuing before you put the waterproofing membrane over it. This is work for a real frame carpenter, but it's pretty doable. The rotted portion has to be taken out and replaced with a like piece of wood. A circular saw can isolate the damaged area of the stud and it can be knocked out with the hammer. Cut and fit a like piece of wood (2" x 4"? 2" x 3"?) in place and secure it with pieces of wood (*the scrap will do just fine*) along the sides of it. We would use a nail gun off the compressor to limit the amount of banging done to the existing walls. Some 2¹/₂" drywall screws also do well, again because there isn't a lot of pounding and banging to the surrounding wall studs. However common 2¹/₂" nails work fine if nothing else is available. Lastly, get some moisture inhibitor . . . it usually can be found in the paint department with the solvents. It's really smelly and usually green in color: get a 2" throwaway (*cheap*) brush, a small tray to put it in . . . and have the windows open and don a respirator if you've got one.

Pencil the amount of surface with the level. Score the wall at the marks with a straight-edge and utility knife or carbide scriber.

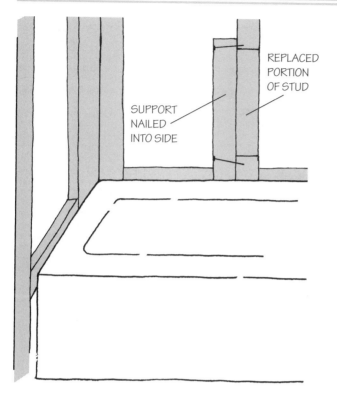

SUPPORT NAILED INTO SIDE

REPLACED PORTION OF STUD

STEP 3 INSTALL ANY STUDDING NECESSARY TO EDGE THE BACKER BOARD. There will have to be studs lining the edge where the backer board will sit, to hold both the backer board and the original wall firmly in place. You may be okay, but if the cut-away wall portion hangs freely—not sharing a stud with the opened wall area—then you'll have to do a bit of carpentry. Use the saber saw to cut the 2" x 4" (*you can also use a regular hand saw, of course, but since you'll be using the saber saw for the backer-board installation, I included it in this Materials Checklist*) and fit them halfway under the wall, showing the other half. Screw through the original wall with drywall screws to hold the new stud in place. Careful, as drywall and plaster at the edge tends to break and crumble easily. ALSO: If there are no horizontal cross-studding

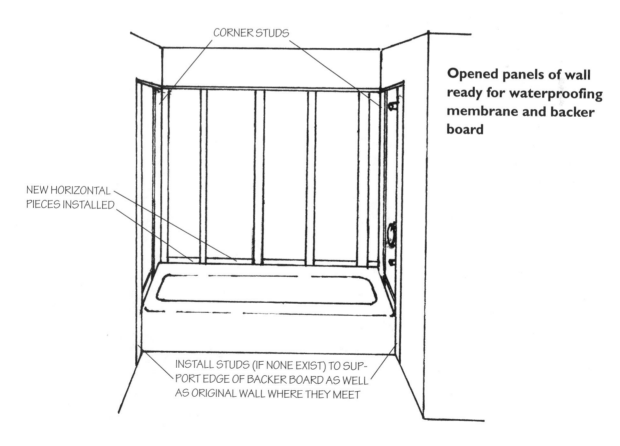

CORNER STUDS

Opened panels of wall ready for waterproofing membrane and backer board

NEW HORIZONTAL PIECES INSTALLED

INSTALL STUDS (IF NONE EXIST) TO SUPPORT EDGE OF BACKER BOARD AS WELL AS ORIGINAL WALL WHERE THEY MEET

at the tub rim, cut and install those pieces. When putting in a cross-stud I generally try to cut each piece so that it is *almost* $1/16$ inch larger than the space and then tap it into place with the hammer, so that it's wedged in nicely.

MARK THE STUDS NOW, WHILE THEY'RE EXPOSED AND EASY TO SEE. Put a small piece of blue painter's tape on the rim of the tub at each stud and one up top on the original wall.

Install the Waterproofing Membrane and Underlayment

MATERIALS CHECKLIST

- [ ] Felt paper, 30 lb.
- [ ] Backer board
- [ ] Staple gun
- [ ] Asphalt gum
- [ ] Straightedge
- [ ] Fiberglass joint tape
- [ ] Respirator
- [ ] Carbide scriber
- [ ] Thinset
- [ ] 5-gallon bucket
- [ ] $1^{5}/_{8}$" screws (*especially for backer board*)
- [ ] Rubber gloves
- [ ] Drill
- [ ] Hole saw kit
- [ ] Drill bit (*slightly smaller than screws*)
- [ ] Bit driver

(Not pictured here: thinset, backer board, or fiberglass tape)

STEP 1 CUT AND INSTALL THE FELT PAPER OVER THE STUDS. Cut and fold the pieces first, using the straightedge and utility knife. Felt paper this thick tends to break when creased cold, so try and heat up each piece folding it (*Maybe near the radiator? In a sauna?*). Trim and staple the two side tub pieces, #1 and #2. Cut the pieces so that there is an extra 2 inches or so that piece #3 can overlap onto. Staple each piece on and put some asphalt gum on the top edges so that when you put the sheets above it it will overlap and sit in the asphalt bed. Use the margin trowel or putty knife. Staple each piece into the studs, one by one taking care to overlap at least 2 inches where there will be a seam. Cut/allow for a flap at the tub edge.

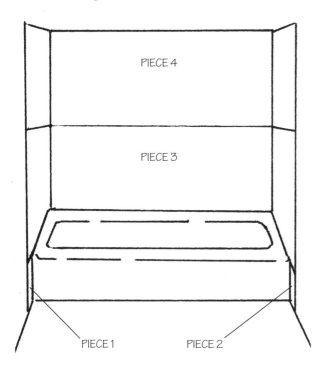

Install the felt paper, folding it first, then gluing each piece at the overlapped portions with asphalt gum

STEP 2 CUT AND INSTALL THE BACKER BOARD PANELS. Put each one in place, pilot the holes for the screws (*drill a hole ahead through the backer board surface with the drill bit*) and fasten the boards to the studs with the $1\frac{5}{8}$" rock screws. Cut to allow a flap of the front membrane of the backer board to come down to the tub edge where possible. Locate where the plumbing fixtures will intersect at the wall, mark the backer board piece, and cut the holes with the drill and hole saw bit.

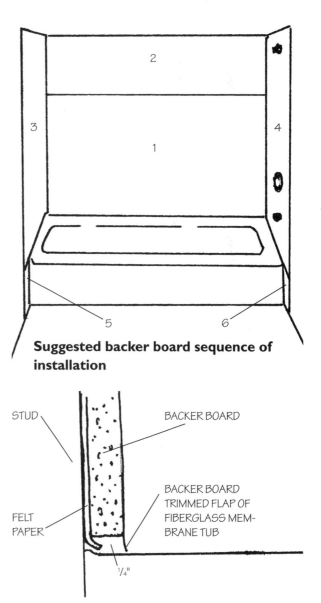

Suggested backer board sequence of installation

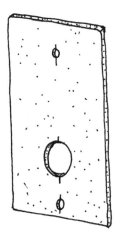

Cut the smaller holes for the plumbing fixtures in the backer board piece with the hole saw of a slightly larger size. Cut the larger one with the saber saw.

STEP 3 FIBERGLASS TAPE THE SEAMS AND TAPE THEM WITH THE THINSET AND FLAT EDGE OF THE TOOTHED TROWEL. Feather the edges while still wet so the taped backer board is somewhat smooth.

Configure Your Layout

MATERIALS CHECKLIST

- [ ] Levels, 48", 24"
- [ ] 1" x 2": 2', 2', 5" strips of wood
- [ ] Handsaw
- [ ] Tile
- [ ] Pencil
- [ ] Spacers
- [ ] Permanent marker

LAY 9 OR 10 TILES STRAIGHT ALONG A LINE, WITH the spacers in place. Use the one of the 3-foot pieces of 1" x 2" wood and mark your jury stick. Use it, in combination with the level, to mark the side and top edges where the tile will stop. Place the level on the back edge of the tub to determine which way it's sloping (*if any*). Same thing on the sides. Determine then where the lowest point of the tub surround at the wall is: place a tile up against the wall there, allow for the spacer, and mark it. Now draw a level line horizontally above the tub on the backer board. Cut and screw in the 5-foot 1" x 2" wood strip at the back wall on the line, as well as one of the 3-foot strips. This will ensure that you start the tile installation *level*. Now use the jury stick to determine where the tile will be set, and mark your grids. Install the last 1" x 2" strip used as the jury stick.

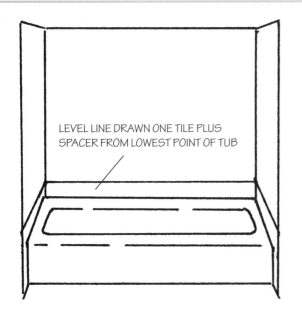

LEVEL LINE DRAWN ONE TILE PLUS
SPACER FROM LOWEST POINT OF TUB

ONE FULL TILE PLUS SPACER

Mark your layout grids for the tile

Cut and Install the Tiles

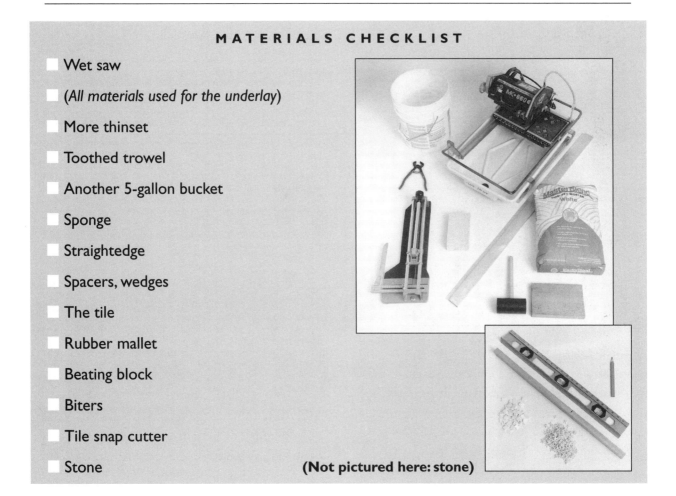

MATERIALS CHECKLIST

- [ ] Wet saw
- [ ] (*All materials used for the underlay*)
- [ ] More thinset
- [ ] Toothed trowel
- [ ] Another 5-gallon bucket
- [ ] Sponge
- [ ] Straightedge
- [ ] Spacers, wedges
- [ ] The tile
- [ ] Rubber mallet
- [ ] Beating block
- [ ] Biters
- [ ] Tile snap cutter
- [ ] Stone

(Not pictured here: stone)

STEP 1 MIX THE THINSET AND SET THE BED IN THE FIRST GRID. Begin setting your tiles on the "shelf" (*1" x 2" wood strips*). Set the spacers in place and move along setting tile, inserting spacers, double-checking the edges with the straightedge, and tapping them in place with the mallet and beating block.

The Voice of Experience

Ready for the soap dish to go in? Set the back wall first, letting the thinset set up just a bit, maybe for 45 minutes or so. Then remove the full tiles from the wall where the soap dish will sit, using your margin trowel. Butter the back of the soap dish and set it in place . . . hold it for a minute or so, and then secure it to the wall with blue painter's tape (*note that the surrounding tile surfaces have to be dry to allow the tape to hold*). Cut and install tile to fit in any surrounding gap.

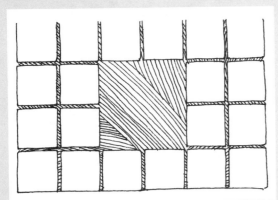

Remove the tiles before the thinset has set and scrape it off the wall. Back-butter the soap dish and set it in place.

STEP 2 CUT THE TILES THAT WILL GO INTO THE CORNER WITH THE SNAP CUTTER. Get ahead and store some up for the length of the wall. REMEMBER: "Soften" (*sand*) any edges of cut tiles before setting them in the thinset bed.

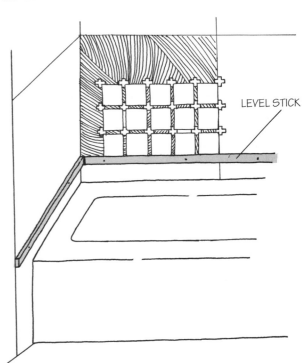

LEVEL STICK

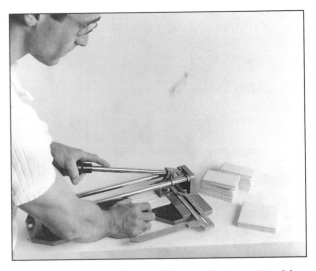

Cut tiles ahead, if possible, as determined by your layout grid

STEP 3 SET THE BORDER BULLNOSE TILES.

STEP 4 REMOVE THE LEVEL WOOD STRIPS (*careful not to loosen the tiles already set at the strips*) AND INSTALL THE TILES AT THE BASE. There should be a space of at least $^1/_8$ inch between the bottom of the tile and the rim of the tub, so use the wet saw to shave each piece individually as you go. You may need to use the wedges to hold these in place to retain the space while the thinset sets.

STEP 5 CLEAN UP THE WET SAW FIRST: EMPTY ITS TRAY AND CLEAN THAT UP. Give the parts a nice sponge bath, as they are all water-resistant. Get a clean bucket of water and place the pump in it, still plugged into the motor. Turn it on for a minute to flush it out cleanly. Scrape all the excess thinset and throw it away in the garbage. Clean the bucket and sponges with water either outside near some rocks, or flush the diluted dirty water down the toilet, and then follow with a couple of flushes to make sure it's all down.

The Voice of Experience

Just as floor tiles that contour around the toilet flange are cut, the odd cuts for the plumbing fixtures can be done on the wet saw. They can also easily be done with the biters. Mark the area to be cut away with the permanent marker, score it if possible with the end of the pick or the utility knife blade. Then "bite" away the area, a bit a time.

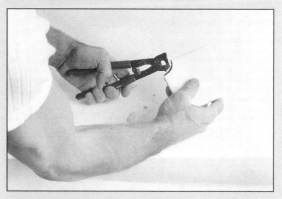

Use the biters to cut tiles that are to go around plumbing fixtures

⊏⊐ Grout

MATERIALS CHECKLIST

- [ ] Two 5-gallon buckets
- [ ] Sponges
- [ ] Margin trowel
- [ ] Latex additive
- [ ] Grout
- [ ] Rubber float
- [ ] Latex gloves
- [ ] Metal pick
- [ ] White rags

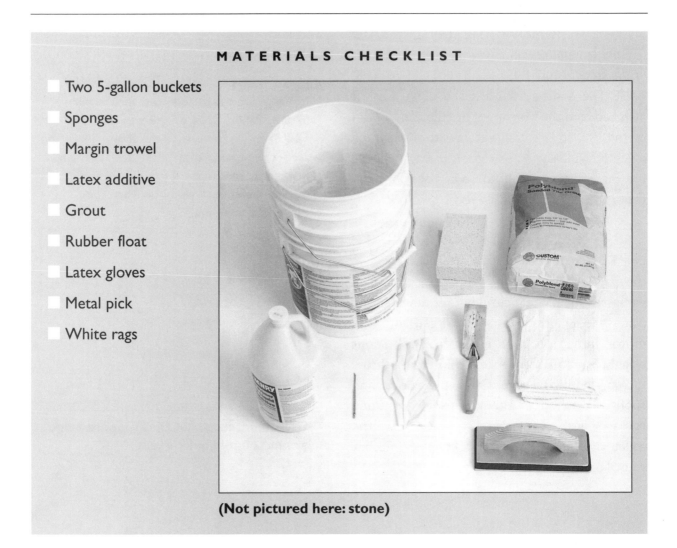

(Not pictured here: stone)

STEP 1 REMOVE THE SPACERS AND CLEAN THE SURFACE OF THE TILE OF ANY LEFTOVER THINSET. Place a strip of blue painter's tape along the space at the tub (*which will be the expansion joint*) to avoid getting grout into it.

STEP 2 GROUT THE TILE USING THE RUB-BER FLOAT. Double-check to make sure the drain is still covered with blue painter's tape. Be sure to fill the crevice between the wall and the bullnose edge tile. I usually take the grout in my hands and fill this by pushing the grout in with my fingers.

STEP 3 WORK A HALF A WALL AT A TIME, GROUTING AND CLEANING EXCESS OFF AS YOU GO ALONG. It's nice that you don't need knee pads this time around: all the work can be done standing up. Still, working on a vertical surface is a different experience, as it takes a bit of practice to get more grout on the wall than down in the tub. Try not to allow too much to linger on the tub bottom . . . keep scooping it back up with the float.

STEP 4 WIPE THE HAZE OFF THE FRONTS OF THE TILE ONCE THE WALLS HAVE BEEN FINISHED, USING A SPONGE AND CLEAN WHITE RAG.

STEP 5 CLEAN UP. Remember, once grout is hard it's almost impossible to remove, even just traces at the bottom of the tub. So wipe clean the inside of the tub as well as all the tools as soon as possible.

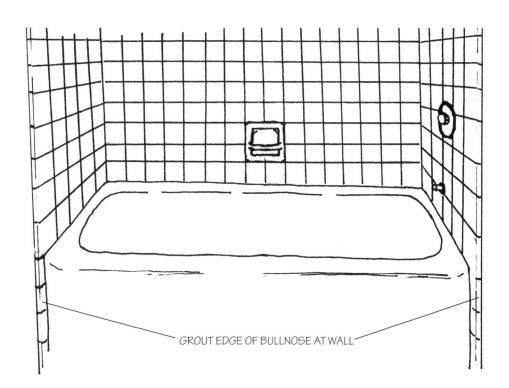

GROUT EDGE OF BULLNOSE AT WALL

CHAPTER 4

Installing Tile on a Kitchen Counter or Bath Vanity

O F ALL THE TILING PROJECTS DONE AROUND the home, this one is my favorite because I don't have to get down on my hands and knees, yet I'm still working on a horizontal plane! The counter sits on what is called the base cabinet (*in kitchens there is the base cabinet—on the floor—and the wall cabinet mounted above them*). Newer counters will probably be one-piece: that is, particle board coated with linoleum. Some may have a separate backsplash piece. Older homes may actually have a mortar bed under a tiled surface. Either way, we're going to get rid of it and start from scratch, or with only the base cabinets sitting intact.

Remove the Old Countertop

F OR THIS PARTICULAR JOB WE'RE GOING TO install tile on a kitchen counter with a backsplash. Doing a bathroom sink vanity counter would involve the same procedure.

First thing to do is to remove the sink. Now, as with the previous tile jobs in this book that involved water sources, if you feel uncomfortable at all working with pipes, especially ones that might be a bit corroded, HIRE A PLUMBER. As it is, one will have to be called in to finish the job (*reinstall the sink/fixtures*).

MATERIALS CHECKLIST

- ☐ *A plumber?*
- ☐ Crescent wrench
- ☐ Monkey wrench
- ☐ Screwdriver
- ☐ 3" rigid putty knife
- ☐ Pry bar
- ☐ Cup or small bucket
- ☐ Rag
- ☐ Hammer
- ☐ Cold chisel
- ☐ Flashlight

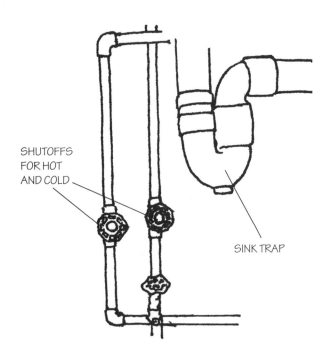

SHUTOFFS FOR HOT AND COLD

SINK TRAP

STEP 1 THE HOT AND COLD VALVES NEED TO BE TURNED OFF UNDERNEATH

THE SINK. This can be done by hand. Then the hoses should be separated from the valves; this can usually be done with a small crescent wrench. A bit of water will seep out once you pull each hose off the valve: keep a rag and cup or small bucket handy and in place.

STEP 2 THE TRAP CAN BE LOOSENED USUALLY BY HAND, IF NOT, BY A LARGE MONKEY (*plumber's*) WRENCH.

STEP 3 NOW FOR THE SINK. Surface mount stainless-steel sinks have small clamps that are tightened under the counter and hold it down. The sink was also probably set in with an adhesive caulk; a bit of shaking/moving and maybe a bit of prying with a rigid putty knife should loosen it enough to separate it from the counter. If it is a porcelain sink, then chances are that it was set originally in an adhesive caulk and the weight of it in the bed of caulk holds it in place.

NOTE: Most plumbers like this procedure for installing a new sink. First he will hook up the new fixtures (*hot/cold, and drain/trap*) to the sink basin *before* it is set in the new counter; the sink then gets set in the new counter; *then* the trap is connected as well as the hot/cold hook-up underneath the sink. If there is also a garbage disposal, it gets done last.

STEP 4 AND NOW THE COUNTER AND ANY BACKSPLASH. Check underneath to find the screws holding the counter down to the base cabinets, using the flashlight. Even after the screws come out, chances are that the counter (*like the sink*) had been set down in some adhesive, which is always a pain the butt to separate. Still, most of the guys I worked with loved this part because it constituted demolition. Use the cold chisel, hammer, and pry bar to get this off. Once you're left with the base cabinets, make sure that all screw and nailheads are removed, too.

The Voice of Experience

NEW COUNTER? Go with a new sink and new fixtures, too. Fully 96% of my clients, when doing a counter redo with tile, have opted to get new fixtures installed: that is, the faucet and hot and cold knobs/handles. The 4% that have wanted to keep the same fixtures (*either to save money or because they liked the look of them*) have had to replace them anyway. I have never installed the exact same fixtures, as they always seem to have corroded a bit. Also, once the client sees the new tile in progress going in, they realize that the old fixtures will look *really* old with the new counter. The same goes with the sink. Even a *new-looking* sink's scratches and wear begin to show up once set against the new tile. And besides, the plumbing stuff underneath: trap, hot and cold hook-ups, will have to be replaced anyway.

⛏ Assess How Much Tile You'll Need (*as Well as the Other Stuff*)

THERE ARE MANY WAYS TO GO AS FAR AS TILE goes (*see the Introduction*). Here we'll use a 4" x 4" field tile, matching V-cap, and surface-mounted bullnose for the backsplash. So besides taking the square footage for the field tile, take the perimeter measurement for the V-cap, and note if there are any outside corner pieces needed for either the V-cap and/or the bullnose border tile.

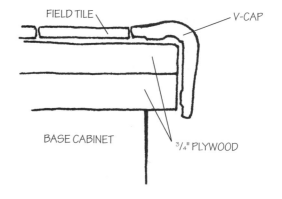

FIELD TILE   V-CAP

BASE CABINET   ³/₄" PLYWOOD

Besides the thinset, grout, and liquid additive, you will also need enough ¾" plywood, 1⅝" deck screws, and CPE (*30 ml chlorinated polyethylene membrane*) to make up the new underlayment. NOTE: Some V-cap pieces require that the counter be built up with two ¾-inch pieces of plywood. If this is the case, get some 1" deck screws along with the additional plywood and other materials.

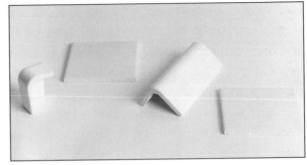

Corner V-cap, bullnose, V-cap, and field tile

Prepare the Surface: Install Underlayment and Waterproofing Membrane

MATERIALS CHECKLIST

- ¾" plywood
- Drill
- Level
- Wood shims
- Deck screws, 1⅝" (*and 1", if double plywood*)
- Bit driver
- Thinset
- Tape measure
- Carpenter's square
- Caulk gun
- 5-gallon bucket
- CPE membrane
- Saber saw
- Circular saw
- Dust mask

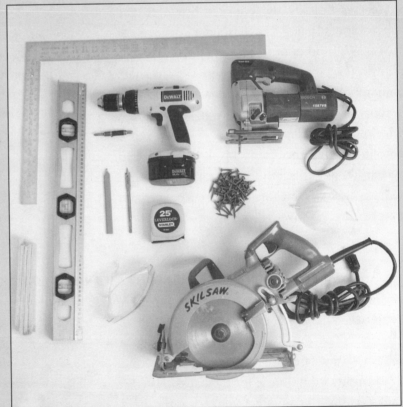

(Not pictured here: backer board, CPE membrane, plywood, thinset, or 5-gallon bucket)

- Goggles
- Toothed trowel
- Pencil
- ½" bore bit
- Staple gun
- Silicone caulk
- Margin trowel

STEP 1 CUT THE PLYWOOD FOR THE COUNTER UNDERLAY. Measure, double-check the squareness with the carpenter's square, and cut with the circular law.

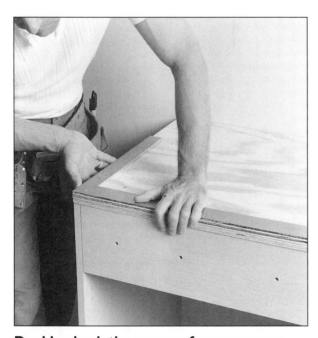

Double-check the corners for squareness

STEP 2 SCREW THE PLYWOOD DOWN TO THE BASE CABINETS. The base cabinets may have gone out of whack (*or never set plumb in the first place*) so place the level on the wood, front-to-back and side-to-side to be sure your new underlay will be level and true. If needed, adjust the plywood level by sticking the wood shims underneath between the base cabinets and the plywood. Use the 1⅝" deck screws to fasten it down to the outside frame of the cabinets that touches the plywood. (*If two layers of plywood are needed, then repeat this step; however, use the 1" deck screws to fasten the top piece to the bottom piece, countersinking the heads just a bit. Put in screws every 6 inches or so and countersink them. The reason for the shorter screws is you want to avoid having the tips popping through from the top sheet to the bottom of the lower sheet . . . you'd be able to feel them by sticking your hands in the drawers later on!*)

STEP 3 CUT THE HOLE FOR THE SINK. Set the new sink in place, centered where it will sit, upside down, and trace around it with the pencil. There will have to be at least a ¼-inch lip for this sink to sit on, so draw a new line just inside the sink line, and this is the line that you'll cut on. Some sinks even come with a template, which can be used and the redrawing of the smaller line

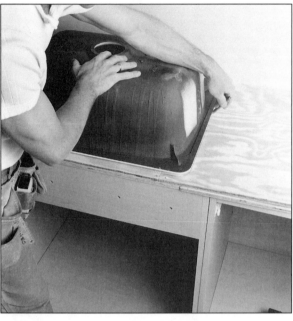

Set the sink upside down on the plywood underlayment and mark it with the pencil

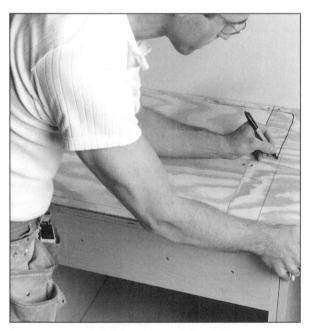

Run a new line with the permanent marker just inside the pencil trace-out of the sink

The Voice of Experience

Gravity doesn't help here. When cutting the hole out of the underlay for the sink often the blade of the saber saw gets jammed when nearing the end of your cut. Also, I'd have to have one of the guys reach under as I finished the cut to catch the piece so it wouldn't fall and scratch the inside of the sink base cabinet. I have seen one of the carpenters I worked with screw a scrap piece of wood across the hole after he had bored the holes and cut the first two parallel sides. Then the final two sides could be cut and the whole piece be lifted out easily when finished.

Drill the corner holes and cut the lengthwise lines; secure a scrap piece of wood across the outline and finish the cut

can be bypassed. Drill four holes, one in each corner, with the bore bit. Now you can get the blade of the saber saw in to cut the shape out.

STEP 4 SET THE WATERPROOFING MEMBRANE IN PLACE. Cut the poly sheeting with the utility knife and straightedge. Cut extra so that it can be folded around the corner of the edges as well as up the backsplash. Fold it now, before the wet stuff comes out. Mix some thinset and trowel a bed for the membrane. The poly can now be set and smoothed down with a straightedge or putty knife. Don't cut the corners: use some more thinset inside the folds and staple them if they don't hold. Put a little of the caulk over the heads of the staples.

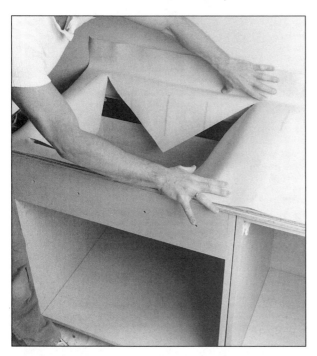

Set and fold the membrane in place first before setting with thinset

STEP 5 CUT THE MEMBRANE INSIDE THE SINK OPENING. Wrap it under the underlay and staple it underneath inside the opening.

The Voice of Experience

What kind of substrate is acceptable tiling the backsplash? Well, since the waterproofing membrane folds up onto the backsplash a few inches, any surface will probably do. Almost. It can't be bumpy, or raw plaster, and if it's unfinished drywall it'll have to be taped, sanded, and primed with an oil-based primer. A smooth, painted surface (*if glossy, then sand it to give it a tooth*) will work fine. If you're unsure of the surface then put a surface of backer board. Use a radius bullnose tile at the edges, which will curve around to the wall and conceal the backer board.

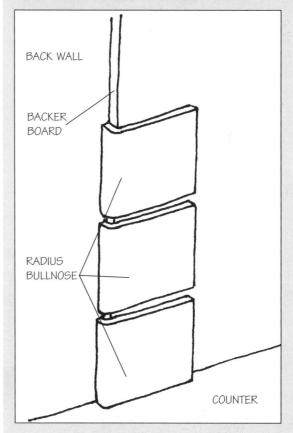

BACK WALL

BACKER BOARD

RADIUS BULLNOSE

COUNTER

Configure Your Layout

MATERIALS CHECKLIST

- ☐ Pencil
- ☐ 24" level
- ☐ The tile: field, V-cap, and bullnose
- ☐ 1" x 2" wood strip
- ☐ Spacers and wedges

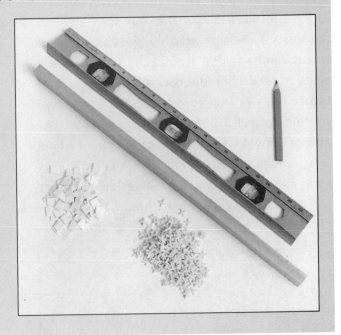

L AY OUT THE FIELD TILES AND MARK THE wood for your jury stick. Turn the piece over and make new marks for the V-cap tile. Decide how you want the tile to sit, in rela- tion to the sink. Keep in mind that if you're using the same size tile on the backsplash that you will want those to line up with the counter rows.

Install the Tile

MATERIALS CHECKLIST

- ☐ Wet saw
- ☐ (All materials used for the underlay)
- ☐ (All materials used for the layout)
- ☐ Additional thinset

- [ ] Another 5-gallon bucket
- [ ] Sponge
- [ ] Straightedge, 48"
- [ ] Spacers, wedges
- [ ] Rubber mallet
- [ ] Beating block
- [ ] Biters
- [ ] Tile snap cutter
- [ ] Stone

(Not pictured here: stone)

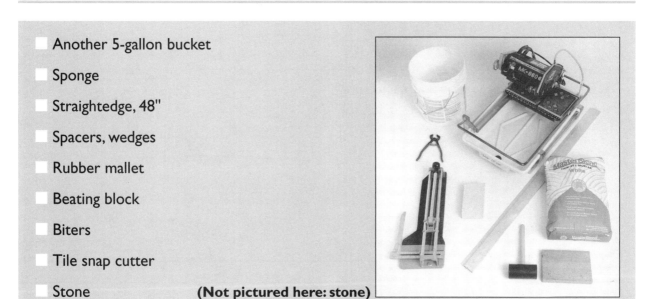

STEP 1 SET THE V-CAP FIRST. Either back-butter each tile and set them in place or trowel on a thinset bed. Even if the cap is sitting in a bed, butter an additional amount for the front lip of the counter edge.

The Voice of Experience

Keep a block of wood on hand that is the same height or taller than the V-cap piece. This will help you get precise cuts when placed under the tile and run under the blade of the wet saw.

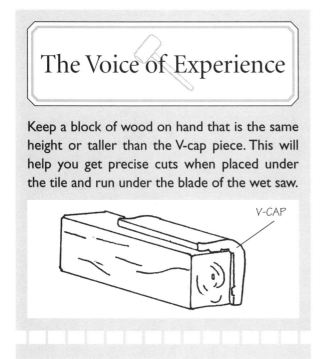

V-CAP

STEP 2 SET THE TILES IN PLACE ON THE COUNTER ACCORDING TO THE LAYOUT GRID. Put in the spacers and give them the beating block/mallet once over as you move along. REMEMBER: "Soften" (*sand*) any edges of cut tiles before setting them in the thinset bed.

STEP 3 CUT THE TILE PIECES FOR AROUND THE SINK. The corners can be trimmed either with the biters or the wet saw.

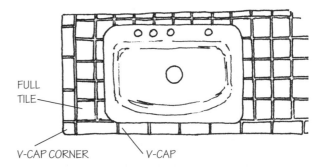

FULL TILE

V-CAP CORNER   V-CAP

Trim the tiles with the wet saw and/or biters to contour to the sink hole cut in the counter. This will create an edge for the sink lip to sit on. NOTE: The front edge of the sink will sit on the V-cap.

STEP 4 SET THE TILES UP THE WALL OF
THE BACKSPLASH. Use the wet saw for any
cuts for the tile to go around any outlet recep-
tacles. Unscrew the receptacle and make sure
the edge of the tile will sit under the metal tip
of the receptacle at the top and bottom.

Grout

MATERIALS CHECKLIST

- Two 5-gallon buckets
- Sponges
- Margin trowel
- Latex additive
- Grout
- Rubber float
- Latex gloves
- Tub/tile adhesive caulk
- Caulking gun
- Metal pick
- White rags

STEP 1 GROUT THE BACKSPLASH AND COUNTER, PUSHING THE GROUT INTO THE SPACES. Make sure to fill the edges, too.

STEP 2 CLEAN THE TILE THOROUGHLY, AS WITH THE OTHER PROJECTS: WIPE THE EXCESS OFF AND AFTER AN HOUR OR SO, USE THE WHITE RAG TO WIPE THE HAZE OFF THE SURFACE.

Two days later after the grout has dried nicely:

STEP 3 SET THE SINK IN PLACE. At this point the fixtures have probably already been installed by a plumber. If not, then take care of that now. The plumber can put the fixtures on, set the sink in a thick bed of tub/tile adhesive caulk (*you've already got it for him*), wipe off the excess, and hook up the stuff underneath.

Finish Up and Repair

 Seal Natural Stone or Slate

MATERIALS CHECKLIST

- [ ] Respirator (*if sealer is oil or petroleum-based*)
- [ ] Applicator pad
- [ ] Paint tray
- [ ] 4" pure bristle brush
- [ ] Sealer
- [ ] Latex gloves
- [ ] White rags

AS STATED IN THE INTRODUCTION, THERE ARE several ways to go with sealing a natural stone. The oil-based one is very, *very* smelly, but as long as a respirator is used to apply it, and you can get out of the house for several hours as it dries, then it can be a superior and lasting sealer. The latex ones are good too, but I always put an extra coat on (*three vs. two*) to make sure I get a good seal. The first coat will get sucked into the porous surface of the tile. The second coat won't as much, so wipe the excess off with a white rag.

Seal the Grout

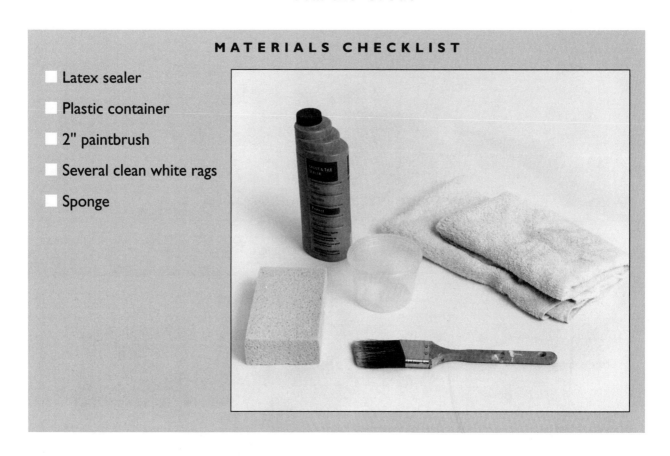

MATERIALS CHECKLIST

- Latex sealer
- Plastic container
- 2" paintbrush
- Several clean white rags
- Sponge

IT NEVER CEASES TO AMAZE ME HOW OFTEN THIS step is skipped by a contractor. The usual excuse is that because the grout was mixed with a latex additive it doesn't need it. The real reason usually is that the installer doesn't want to have to return to the job 3 days (*72 hours*) later and do this final step.

First, give the tile surface one more wipe with a damp sponge and wipe it dry with a rag. Wait a few hours (*for any water residue from the damp sponge to evaporate completely*). Apply the sealer directly to the grout with the paintbrush. Follow the directions for a wait time, and then wipe the excess off the tile surface with the rag. Like the sealant for tile surfaces, the grout sealer will also get absorbed nicely on the first coat. You can usually follow with a second coat in an hour or so, and not as much of this one will soak into the grout. That's good: it means the grout is getting sealed. I almost always do a THIRD COAT. It can't hurt, and it'll probably help make the grout keep its color for that much longer.

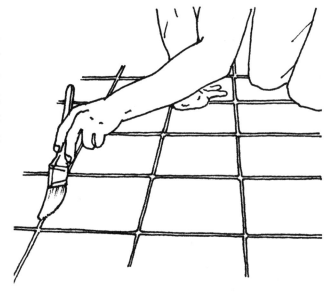

Apply the latex sealer to the grout with the sash brush

Caulk the Expansion Joints

MATERIALS CHECKLIST

- [ ] Compressible foam strips
- [ ] Utility knife
- [ ] Straightedge
- [ ] Caulk gun
- [ ] 3" putty knife
- [ ] Latex gloves
- [ ] Caulk
- [ ] Sponge
- [ ] Mineral spirits (*if the caulk is 100% silicone*)

The crevices left from each job

•the perimeter of a floor at the walls and/or base cabinet

•the inside corners of the tub walls

•where the tub meets the tile

•where the counter meets the backsplash

will have to be filled with a caulk (*vs. grout*) to allow for some movement during temperature changes, which occur with the building materials on and under the substrate, as described earlier. I like working with the tub/tile caulks available, as they generally come in a variety of colors and are water-based, so easy to work with.

Nevertheless, there are some colored 100% silicone caulks, and since this is much more lasting solution I'd recommend it.

Push in the strips of compressible foam with the putty knife (*see the Introduction for diagram of an EXPANSION JOINT*). With the utility knife slice the excess to at least ⅛ inch below the level of your grout line. Squeeze the caulk into the crevice, wipe the excess off with a finger, then wipe the excess off with a rag dipped in mineral spirits. Sometimes I dip my latex-glove-covered finger in the mineral spirits and smooth it that way. Additional areas that need caulking but not necessarily compressible foam are: **where the sink sits on the tiled counter, where the tile meets the bathtub/shower fixtures, where the toilet meets the tiled floor.**

The Voice of Experience

CAULK THE TUB IN YOUR BATHING SUIT (*OR BIRTHDAY SUIT*). When you're ready to caulk the tub where it meets the wall, before removing the blue tape, *fill the tub with water.* Better make it warm. Now remove the tape. Get the caulk, gun, and sponge, take off your clothes, and sit in the tub. You're going to caulk (*and let the caulk dry*) while there is water in the tub, which translates to *weight.* By putting the caulk in the crack while you are in the tub with water, you're doing it when there is the most amount of weight there ever will be in. As the caulk dries with the water (*weight*) still in the tub, it will be better able to contract as necessary once the tub is emptied. If the caulking is done with the tub empty and then someone goes to take a bath later on, there's a greater risk that the caulk will separate from the tub, as it dried in the contracted position. My Mom taught me this one, and though I've never heard of another contractor doing it, it makes perfect sense to me. Although one would hope that a tub sitting in place won't move with weight, you never know: taking into account the movement of wood (*floor joists*) throughout the seasons. And besides, it not only can't hurt, but it's kind of fun. You can also do the corners up the walls at this point, too.

CAULK

CAULK

CAULK

Upkeep: Resealing Annually

I HAVE SOME CLIENTS IN CALIFORNIA NAMED JON and Michelle Blieberg who have me do just this once a year. I've told all of my clients actually, after doing a tile job, that it would help the grout retain its color if the sealing was redone on an annual basis. I've even tried to teach them how to do it themselves, but I think the Bliebergs are the only ones who've paid any attention to me. Jon originally bought the additional sealer, but, because he is always so busy, he has always had me do it when I come to work on other projects.

You want to be sure that the floor and grout are as clean as you can get them first. A *tiny* bit of muriatic acid mixed with water could do the trick, but that stuff is pretty caustic, even in small quantities. Usually the tile surface can be cleaned with some kind of cleanser and then the grout cleaned out with warm water and a toothbrush. Be sure it's completely dry now, before starting the sealer. If you seal in the not-completely-dry grout it may appear blotchy or discolored. When you're ready to seal it, just follow the directions in the "Sealing the Grout" section above.

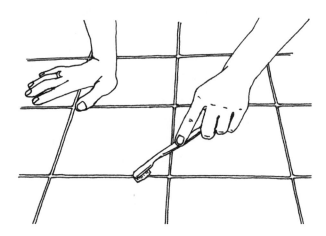

Broken Tile on a Finished Job?

I T'S PRETTY EASY TO POP A DAMAGED TILE OUT of the thinset bed, if it's been sitting just a few days. But after a week or so the thinset begins to cure, and if the cracked or broken tile has to come out of an old tile job, then figure it ain't gonna be easy. But it's doable.

MATERIALS CHECKLIST

- Hammer
- Goggles
- Tile(s) replacement
- Spacers, or cardboard bits
- Blue painter's tape

- Grout replacement
- Cold chisel
- Thinset
- Margin trowel
- Sponge

Broken tile is sharp, so take care when proceeding with this. Wear your goggles. Score the front of the tile and begin to break it away by tapping the cold chisel at the tile surface with the hammer. Be careful not to pound too hard as you could loosen nearby tiles . . . sometimes this is unavoidable, so don't get too exasperated if it happens. Scrape out the surrounding old grout as well as the exposed bed of thinset. Mix up some new thinset, back-butter the tile(s) with the margin trowel, and set the tile in place. Use cardboard bits to space it properly, if you don't have any of the original spacers. Run some blue painter's tape over the tile to hold it in place. Return the next day and grout it.

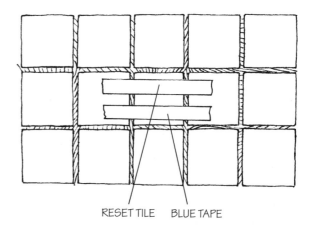

RESET TILE   BLUE TAPE

Mix a small batch of thinset for a loose tile, reset it and mask it down

GLOSSARY

acid wash: a cleaning of materials with acid and water, usually refers to muriatic acid on stone

applicator pad: flat, absorbent surface used with handle to apply liquids like paint, polyurethane, and tile sealers; available in various sizes

asphalt gum: black solvent-based paste used as an adhesive in situations that require water resistance

backer board: sand and cement sheets sandwiched between two layers of fiberglass tape; designed and used as a tile substrate

backsplash: wall portion directly above counter on base cabinet

base cabinet: cabinets installed on the floor, usually in a kitchen or bath; with a counter and/or sink installed level on top

beating block: piece of wood used to set tiles flush in relation to one another

bed: newly combed layer of thinset or mortar for tiles to be set in

bit driver: used in a drill to drive in screws, usually a Phillips head

carbide scriber: forged metal tool used to score cementous materials for the purpose of cutting/breaking; specifically backer boards

carpenter's square: flat measuring tool manufactured with a true 90-degree angle

caulk: soft toothpastelike material, sold in tubes and available in a variety of colors and bases, used to fill cracks and holes; solidifies after application

chalk line: a mark of chalk on a surface left from the positioning of a line reel held in a straight line

china marker: wax marking tool

closet bolt: sits in a pair pointed up from flange and, together with the bolt, holds the toilet to the floor

cold chisel: usually thicker and denser than a wood chisel; used as a prying instrument or cutting of cementous materials in tandem with a hammer

compressible foam: soft material used to fill part of an expansion joint

CPE (chlorinated polyethylene): a thick layer used as waterproofing membrane in a tile substrate installation

cure: the process of an applied material to completely *dry*; measured by time, as in the length of time it takes for an epoxied or solvent-based caulk or mastic to oxidize, or for all the water in a latex-based caulk, mastic, grout, or mortar to evaporate

expansion joint: a space left at a meeting point of two different building materials, for the purpose of allowing each to move independently of each other

firing: the action of putting bricks, tiles, or other building materials under high temperatures to make them more dense

float, rubber: flat tool with handle used to install wet grout in tile joints and spaces

float, wooden: flat wood surface with handle used to smooth wet building materials, such as mortar, cement, or thinset

float strip: piece of wood set in mortar bed for the purpose of packing/dragging (*screeding*) the mud into a level plane

granite: a very dense, natural stone

grout: pastelike material used to fill crevices and spaces between set tiles

grout haze: film that appears on tile surface after grouting has been cleaned initially

hammer, claw: basic hammer with a curved claw for removing nails, about 13" long

joint tape: paper or fiberglass strips used

joist: support of a structure that runs horizontally and to which the floor and/or ceiling are affixed; run parallel every 8" to 16"

jury stick: a straight edge of wood or metal marked with the measurements of tile and spaces in a layout of a tile job

latex additive: milky water-based bonding agent used in place of water to mix mortar, thinset, and grout; also used as a primer over other building materials (*like drywall, linoleum, or painted walls*) for adhesives

latex sealer: water-based penetrating liquid used to seal grout and tiles

layout: the planned positioning of tiles, marked on the substrate for the installation

level: an imaginary line or plane joining two points of equal height

marble: soft, natural stone, usually sold with basic sealed surface

mastic: adhesive

mastic, cement-based: mortar or thinset adhesive

mortar: cement-based adhesive

mortar bed: the traditional substrate constructed and installed by tile setters consisting of sand, cement, wire, and/or waterproofing membrane (*felt or tar paper, or poly sheeting*)

mosaic: any tile pieces smaller than 1" used with other similar-sized tiles or various colors to create a design or picture

mud: a tradesman's reference to the sand, cement, and water (*or liquid additive*) mixture used to make a mortar bed

muriatic acid: highly caustic and vaporous liquid used to clean building materials, as in newly set tile with dried thinset on the surface

nonvitreous: high absorption of water; refers to building materials that can take 7% and over

non-wet installation: a tile job that sits or will sit in an area that will not need to have any water resistance

paddle: long metal mixing tool used with drill to blend/mix mortar, thinset, and grout

plumb: an exactly vertical imaginary line

polyethylene: plastic sheeting used as a waterproofing membrane in a tile substrate

pony wall: a small peninsula-shaped portion of a wall that protrudes into the room, usually as a divider that does not go all the way up to the ceiling

poultry netting: also known as "chicken wire," sheets of metal mesh used as part of the substrate of a mortar bed

pry bar: metal tool with curved flattened end, used as a wedge to aid in prying building materials apart; also acts as a claw for removing spikes and nails

reducer: piece of building material used as edge to an unfinished end of flooring, usually one of a different height than the floor surface it meets

rubber mallet: "hammer" with hard rubber head and handle, used for any pounding needed when there is a worry that a hammer will damage the surface

sash brush: paintbrush with the bristles cut at an angle

saw, flush cut: fine-toothed handsaw with arm attached at different level from blade to allow close cuts (through door casing straight along at the floor, for instance)

saw, hole: serrated metal circular bit used to cut holes in building materials

saw, hypoid or circular: hand-held power tool usually with a 7¼" round blade

saw, saber: power tool with small blade that can cut shapes and angles in building materials; also called orbital or "jig" saw

saw, wet: power tool used to cut tile; pump and motor keep blade wet when in motion

saw, worm drive: also called hypoid saw; circular saw

score: to mark a surface of a material with a sharp tool with the intention of breaking or cutting the material at that point

screed: the action of smoothing the packed mud, with a straight edge moved in a back-and-forth motion between two stationary planes

scribe: to mark for notation or measurement

sealant: usually refers to caulk or mastic that, when applied and dried, prevents moisture from damaging surrounding building materials

shim: to bring out a surface by means of some material, such as a strip of wood or metal placed under a toilet to make it level

sink trap: the curved metal pipe connecting the sink drain to the drainpipe

slake: blending that grout does as it sits after initial mixing

snap cutter: a hand tool with a handle and scoring blade that is used to run a single line across the surface of tile and then break it at that point

spacer: a plastic or rubber piece shaped like a cross, to sit between newly set tiles in their bed, to hold them in a specific place until the tiles set

stone: used to sand a cut edge of a tile to make it less sharp

straightedge: any flat tool with true straight edge; used as a measuring and setting aid in tiling; usually made of metal or wood

subfloor: the surface between the finished floor and the joists

substrate: the general term to encompass any or all of the materials set for the tiles to be installed upon

tar paper: comes in various width rolls and is used as a waterproofing membrane of a tile job substrate

Teflon tape: white tape wrapped around threads of many plumbing fixtures before they are attached to water source for the purpose of sealing connection for water leakage

thick bed: the traditional tile substrate installed for levelness, waterproofing, and durability, consisting of sand, cement, wire, and a waterproofing membrane

thin bed: commonly used tile substrate today, consisting of backer board and/or plywood and/or a waterproofing membrane

thinset: the adhesive used for thin-bed installations

tile, base: trim tile used on wall at floor in place of a wooden base molding; usually in bathrooms

tile biters: plier-shaped tool with sharp cutting ends, used to break ceramic tile

tile, bullnose: trim tile with curved/finished edge

tile, cement-bodied: tiles made from mixture of cement, sand, and water either pressed or rolled for their shape

tile, field: the majority of the tiles set in an area, not including the border or perimeter tiles

tile, glazed: second firing seals a coating on the surface of the tile, making it water-resistant

tile, quarry: generally unglazed "natural" (*not machine-made*) tiles

tile, radius bullnose: trim tile with curved edge designed to sit on edge of backer board and cover edge; coming flush to original surface

tile, Saltillo: cement-bodied pressed tile named after the town in Mexico where they originate

tile, trim: the boarder or perimeter tiles of an application

tile, unglazed: single-fired tile that is "raw" and needs sealing once installed

toilet flange: plate on floor that sits over 4" toilet drain; made of concrete, steel, or plastic and the closet bolts sit in it

trowel, buttering: flat, small, pointed-bladed tool used to apply small amounts of mortar or thinset to a building material

trowel, margin: flat, small, rectangular-bladed tool used to mix building materials

trowel, plain: flat metal hand tool with straight edges; used to smooth or apply mortars or mastics

trowel, toothed: flat metal hand tool with squared or pointed teeth on two edges; used to apply bed of mastic/mortar/thinset for tile

try square: measuring tool manufactured with true 90-degree angle

underlayment: general term referring to the layer/layers under the finished floor

utility knife: handle holding single-edged blade, used for shaving, cutting, scribing, and scoring building materials

V-cap: edge piece of tile used on counters

vitreous: low level of water absorption; between zero and 3%

waterproofing membrane: a layer installed with the substrate of a tile job; tar paper and CPE are examples

wax ring: membrane designed to sit on bottom hole of toilet and seal it to flange hole in floor

wedge: a plastic or rubber piece used to sit between newly set tiles to hold them in a specific place

wet installation: a tile job that sits or will sit in an area that will be exposed to water; such as a kitchen counter, bath floor, or tub/shower walls

wrench, crescent: smaller and easier to handle than monkey wrench, is also used to unscrew pipes, usually ¼" and up

wrench, plumber's "monkey": large, easily recognized wrench used to unscrew pipes with threading of 1½" or more

INDEX

NOTES

NOTES

NOTES